Everything Changed

Growing up is a wonderful thing to do

Charlotte Eriksson
The Glass Child

Everything Changed When I Forgave Myself

Journals & Poems

Growing up is a wonderful thing to do

***

Charlotte Eriksson
www.CharlotteEriksson.com
www.BrokenGlassRecords.se

Cover artwork by Zukellogs
instagram.com/zukellogs

DISCOGRAPHY

Charlotte Eriksson EP, *2011*
This Is How Ghosts Are Made EP, *2011*
Songs of An Insomniac EP, *2011*
I'd Like To Remain A Mystery, LP *2013*
Empty Roads & Broken Bottles: in search for The Great Perhaps, book 2013
I'd Like To Remain A Mystery *Acoustic Edition*, 2013
Love Always, Your Tragedy EP, 2013
I Must Be Gone and Live or Stay and Die, LP 2014
Another Vagabond Lost To Love, book 2015
You're Doing Just Fine, book 2015
Under Northern Skies, *LP* 2016
This Silence Now EP, 2017
Coming Home EP, 2017
Everything Changed When I Forgave Myself, book 2018

Overview

PREFACE

This is a story from lost to found. This is a journey of a wandering youth, trying to find a place in the world, to slowly growing into a peaceful meditation on the joys of growing up, changing and befriending yourself.

If you feel young and lost, searching for something, know that the search is not for nothing. Rejections will redirect you to more exciting roads. When you think your life is falling apart, it's usually falling together in disguise. Your search will throw you on journeys you never would have dreamt of, in your mind and in the world. It will make you delve deeper into this spirit of yours, and you will be a better, more conscious human being for not ignoring your questions. They're trying to lead you somewhere … follow them. Rainer Maria Rilke wrote that you must live the questions. Don't seek answers you're not ready to receive yet: live the mystery and enjoy the unfolding of yourself.

There is a peace so profound that nothing can disturb it. I know, because I've felt it, though briefly—I know it exists. I used to be scared that if I gave up my sadness, I wouldn't be me anymore. But growing into a peaceful state of mind does not mean happy ever after. It means that you can now feel the sadness, but not let it consume you. Watch it, feel it, learn from it, create from it, but don't let it consume you.

This story starts with me, in a city (any city), lost and alone (as I spent my youth), to slowly growing into my age, accepting my path and finding the adult me I feel proud to be. My elegies transition into hopeful meditations on all the simple joys of life, and how lovely it feels to befriend myself. *Part 1* is my melancholy, *Part 2* is my peace.

I hope you will read those pieces in different places, through different phases of your life, and I hope they can make you feel something.

Love always,
Charlotte

Journal I

January 2017

by the water….

I am alone, as I've always been, as I've started every book and song and chapter I've ever written, and I am facing the sea, as I always end up doing. I was born for the ocean, for the road, and I longed to build my reputation as a fearless nomad, forever roaming the country with a suitcase and my guitar. Light as the wind itself, a romantic mystery passing through people's lives, leaving them with moments of magic, wondering where I might be now.

But the shift goes slow and if I had the choice I'd move into that little red house on the corner of the street, where I used to go and drink at night, and I'd build a home inside, by the fireplace. Big, red candles, a double bed with the same kind of pillows you get at really nice hotels, and I would always have people over. Friends and strangers, invited for wine, dinner, breakfast, and I'd make it a place to come for everyone. Where they could tell their stories, share their worries or joys, and I'd listen and understand; pour another coffee, wine, whisky, and end the night with another song, all together, all as one. "Let's put music to our troubles…"

But I am alone as I've always been. As I've started every book and song and chapter I've ever written, and there is no house to come home to. Last year I poured the booze down the drain, bought a desk and threw the books in a cartoon box. I wanted new influences —clean living and no more blurry memories of nights with strangers but still alone. I'd had enough of homeless travelling just to feed my art and I wanted stability and comfort; a calm sense of existence. I wanted a friend, a hand to hold, arms to fall asleep in. I set the box of books on fire, replaced them with sophisticated recipes and bought clean clothes. I went to the hair dresser, joined a gym, a yoga studio, got a local bus pass. I enrolled in a course to learn German, then psychology, then history… I could learn stuff! I could develop and reinforce the pride I once had. I still had time to be fully equipped for daily life.

You turn so vague on the road, always erasing and shaping, replacing sides you no longer wish to have with new ones to explore, and you turn so worn. My feet still look like stones, as they grow after years of walking, and I hide my hands in gloves. It gets better though, we're flexible creatures, able to turn and flex in any shape we please and it's never too late to reshape, but it takes time … and effort … and patience … Things that are virtues and nothing to take for granted, like I've done, and now I'm restlessly stomping my feet in the basement where I pay my rent.

I am alone, as I've always been, as I've started every book and song and chapter, and I am facing the sea, as I always end up doing.
Another book about leaving? Another book about searching? Another book about love lost and friends gone and where to go now?

No, not this time.
This is a story of ways gone right. Ways gone absolutely right, for once.

This is my journey from lost to found.

XX X

If I could say anything to 17-year-old me, it would be this:

this is a lot harder than i thought.
also,
this is a lot more beautiful than i thought.

and maybe even:
You, are a lot more beautiful than you think.

PART ONE

The Loneliest Girl In The World

Journal II

ON THE RUN....

In this story I am nothing else than what I appear to be. I'm not me, the Author, I'm me, the Character. I float from city to city with no end in sight, no goal or clearer vision other than not giving up—not stopping. They told me I would do great things, that I could "be something". But I got scared and grew up and detached myself from everyone I've ever known and now I'm running lonely and free in the night, pretending I hear wolves and see the moon but mostly I'm looking over my shoulder, scared of angry men following me with evil inside.

In this story I am lost, just as I want to be, I think. Picture a big city, never asleep, always screaming. Cars speeding at 3 a.m. and there is a loud bass piercing through the summer night from a club by the corner. Pretty youths stumbling out in high heels and designer jeans, laughing and taking photos they will laugh at even more tomorrow. Picture me, walking with a rucksack, hands in my pockets, headphones on and a thick beanie tucked over my head to not feel so open, so seen.

In this story we will come back to the city over and over again. Which city on which continent doesn't matter, it's a city like every other and I don't know it more than I know every street in every city like the back of my hand because I've walked them back and forth, up and down, summers and winters. We will come back to the concrete, the busy streets, the early mornings. We will try to escape it. We will try to settle in, find a calmer pace and pick fresh flowers in the morning somewhere quiet and lovely.

But our heroine is the loneliest of us all, by choice, maybe. But mostly because of an unsettled worry and an undying love for all things free, so she hid and kept quiet. Stayed as light as could be, never owning more than necessary, always knowing the fastest way to the exit. Now it's a habit, too strong to break and it's hard to make people care again once you've taught them not to. It's hard to tell people that you need them, once you've told them you don't.

That's all you need to know for now:
1. Our heroine is lost with no plans or future or safety net to fall down on.
2. Our heroine is the loneliest heroine in the world. So lonely her death would take days to discover and even then no one would know how to celebrate her life because who knew her? Who kept in touch? Who wanted to know?

Every story needs a plot. We need a conflict, something that hinders our heroine from getting what she wants, and we need a hero's journey. Her, going off in the world to chase after something material, stumbling in the dark, rearranging to find something spiritual, and we need her homecoming. People waving from the distant shore, greeting her home.

Unless in this story there is no heroine (only me, who's anyone, all of us, really), and there is no plot (only many small ones and a sharp dream), and there are too many conflicts to make them count one by one and my homecoming didn't happen.

I'm still on the run.

Every character needs to be driven by something. You need to give her a clear persona. Something she's standing for. You need to give her a favorite colour, interests, beliefs and manners. What is she looking for? What is she running from? What does she think of her name? Who's her best friend? Is she scared of flying? What's her IQ? Does she have a weird tic she can't stop, like blushing or mumbling or fiddling with her necklace when she gets nervous?

I remember a super moon, so big and clear it made me wish for a lot more and it lit up the sky like nothing was ordinary. It's those moments, those goddamn moments, that keep me running. A line in a book, jumping straight off the page, shooting me off in a different direction; a conversation with a stranger sparking up a new idea and I run with it; an hour with the moon and the gods, negotiating my fate.

There are no people to call. There is no love in the morning. There is a huge respect for literature and bright minds. Joseph Campbell, Jack Gilbert, Etty Hillesum, Chekhov... The list goes on and there is an undying love for all things wonderful, all things magic. All things lovely and tragic, intelligent or sad, but in this story, these are the things that keep our heroine lost. These are the things that make her go on and on, endless views with no end in sight, and this is the magic curse that makes her burn up the letters and throw keys in rivers. These are the things that keep her running. From what? Who knows. But run she does.

In this story our heroine is not me, the Author, but an idea. I know she's real, running lonely through the fields escaping the council. Maybe it's you? Maybe you don't believe me. Maybe it's me … Maybe it's all of us, at some point.

Either way, this is a story.
This is my story.

Let us start by the water...

He asked, “Where are we going?”
I said, “We're just going.”

I wouldn't change a thing

"There's a sadness in your eyes," they say. "It makes me look away".
I smile and nod and turn around, taking the long way home
wondering where home is, what Dave is doing tonight,
if my old school teacher is doing alright
and what did that critic mean about that song of mine?
The sky is dark blue and this road is so empty.
I miss my friends (can I still call them friends?)
and I miss my home (can I still call it home?)
and I miss my granddad and my old band, Tuesday nights at the pub
and Sunday mornings on a train
to nowhere I never knew
but I miss it.
and I miss waking up with a hand in my hand,
the front porch alone, or watching him smoke,
and I miss being the youngest at the party.
everyone asking my name
and I miss feeling fearless and brave, no words could touch me
and I miss a lot of things...

but I also wouldn't change a single thing.

I wouldn't go back, one second of my life,
for I made this body and mind all on my own, with nothing but will and force
and I refused to give in when that's all I really wanted to do
and I've been tired and bored, frustrated and angry (just wanting someone to blame) and I think I'm the loneliest of them all, no one to see or call

… but I smile all the time. I laugh all the time. Loud; that real one from your belly and after a minute you take a deep breath and you feel energy in every vein of your body, happy for having a reason to laugh like this, like that,
and I've heard the loveliest of voices singing words that felt like home
and I'm being met with open arms by people who invite me home, to them, and they hug me and smile, saying "thank you for coming".
I feel love and loved; warmth towards all
and I wouldn't change a thing. I got it all.

There is sadness in my eyes and my chest tightens up sometimes, but I'm so happy. I'm so happy.

I wouldn't change a thing.

Amsterdam

I've built my home in cities I've never been to, dreaming away by the breakfast table, clicking on flat ads and imagining moving. I find my safety in the thought that I could move, go anywhere, start over and anew and this time I'll get it right. I'll keep my head above water. I'll write and create, find friends and go to fancy dinners on Wednesday evenings. Drink martinis until four in the morning and discuss the state of affairs with someone I don't know that well but we wouldn't mind because we would have no hurry with it: we would not be temporary leavers, we would be staying.

Not often do the cities live up to my daydreams, and that's not why I go there either. I wander and I gaze, pretending that I live there, for just a day or two. I enter bookshops and cafés, read and write and—for a short while—I feel at home.

But then I get a little slumbery, and bored, and I go home because I have things to do and my bed and a routine, a contract and rent to pay but it's okay, it's okay, it's all okay, I tell myself.

Amsterdam welcomed me with open arms and a blue sky. The sky is never blue in Hamburg and I haven't seen the stars in so long. People were friendly and smiled, started conversations in a language I could understand and no one was annoyed by my mere existence. Accepted, I guess you could call it, maybe as a tourist but I think even more because people were interested in where I came from, what my plan was and why my voice sounded strained.
"Just a cold," I smiled. "Trains are rough."

I'm so young but I've started feeling like I'm too old to keep running, starting over and moving places. It would feel so nice to start something with the intention of keeping it. To build something proper. Carefully from the ground because I would want it to last, this time, now, after all these years. I would repair and fix, instead of throwing away and replacing, buying something new, and I would like to know what it feels like to call someone my person. I would like to know what it feels like to have someone call me his friend, by name, on the phone, just kind of simply asking what I'm up to, if I want to come over. *Some wine and a record, whatd'ya think?*

Home. I keep calling places my home and I keep writing about it. Trying to dissect and figure out, because it seems that everyone around me has built their homes on stable ground. They have all they need and they got through the youthful years of chaos and mess and they're all fine now. Calm and secured, elegantly holding someone's arm in photographs and they wear jewellery and classy shoes.

In the meantime I drink black coffee and read Rimbaud. In cafés, on trains, in the basement where I think I live and nothing makes me happier than writing beautiful little sad songs. So sad it tears my chest up when I write it because it's just so fucking lonely and it's so unbelievably lovely. Preferably in the morning so I can enjoy the feeling of having created something for as long as I can! The absence of music is so very loud.

I wouldn't change it. I wouldn't trade this for the world. My own still existence, with space and silence and freedom to do as I please. But I would simply like to try something new out. Try a different way of feeling. Maybe not so small. Maybe not so forgotten. Maybe a little special, even?

I don't know. I simply liked it here. Amsterdam was kind to me and I stayed up counting the stars last night. They shone like bright lights through my window, and around 2 a.m. the snow started to fall. It was quite a lovely view and I breathed it in like I only do when I truly love something, and there was a small sadness creeping in through my chest because I knew I would have to leave it, go back to my basement with no stars in sight. But I pushed it aside because those moments are rare and I'm happy because now I know this place exists and that's all you need sometimes. You need to know that lovely places exist and you can go there, when things go wrong, and it's a place of solace.

I build my home in cities, and it's quite a lovely thing.

Lonely hotel nights

Lonely hotel nights. Where do you go when you can go anywhere? I could wander these streets, this city, have a drink with the man at the bar downstairs. I could ask someone for help. Ask for company. I could hug my mum and say "I love you". Fall in love with a pretty boy, go away, make it big, be a star.

Where do you go when you can go anywhere?

Your Constellation

You will find yourself wanting to leave and go home at the same time, and there is nothing you can do about this. You will find yourself feeling too large for your body, and at the same time find yourself with a body that feels too large for you, and there is nothing you can do about this. You will find yourself with a beautiful boy and you will not want to stay in that room, with him, even though there is nothing more you can ask for in another human being, and there is nothing you can do about this.

There is a constellation in the sky that was created the very second you were born, because no one and nothing was in the exact same position between the moon and the stars at the time of your birth, and this is your place in the universe. This is your spot to stand up tall because no one else was made for it, no one could have been, and neither will anyone else ever be made for it, and so you will just have to stay.

You don't want to. I know. You want to inhabit others' successes and luck and they're smiling and building wonderful lives with people all around and you want to walk in their footsteps. You want to leave your own spot, your own place. You want to do it now. You've had enough.

You will make a plan and pack your rucksack one night when the time is right, and you will say you'll be gone for a while, maybe come back, maybe not. You will choose a new name, a new haircut, dress yourself in all the clothes you've seen your heroes wear and you will inhabit a new character. You will sip coffee in secondhand cups at cafés in cities where people don't notice you and no one asks if you cut your hair or if you've seen Sarah lately.

You will find people you'd like to call your friends but you will also notice that interactions are hard when the time won't last and you will only go so deep until someone says "let's just get another drink" and you will walk home alone or with people you can't remember the names of, in the morning, but he was kind and took his shoes off in the entrance.

Back to your constellations; the only place you can inhabit.

There is a path that is yours to walk and maybe yours is where you stand right now, but maybe it's not? Maybe you feel out of place, out of town, out of mind, out of luck, because you simply slipped too far away from your spot and you just need to find your way back again. Don't rush so much. Ease into it. You're on foreign ground, that's why you feel so uncertain, so unsure. Look up, there's a whole world out there to explore, and you have your own place in it. Isn't it exciting?

There are things that will happen to you and there is nothing you can do about this.

You will say goodbye to someone you love, and someone you love will say goodbye to you; that he just does not love you anymore,
and there is nothing you can do about this. You will lose your credit card on the subway and you will have to walk home in the dark, with no money, and you will panic for a second and maybe call your father, cry, tell him you want to come home;
and there is nothing you can do about that.
Things will happen on that spot you inhabit and this is good, this is fine, this is all planned. Ease into it. Don't rush so much. Nothing

ever lasts, nothing ever stays. It's exciting, isn't it? Exciting beyond belief.

There are things that will happen to you and there is nothing you can do about this.
Isn't it exciting beyond belief?

Passive naiveté

I'm tongue-tied. I'm a kaleidoscope. You can flex and turn and shift the angles and you will find different shades of me depending on the mood
the weather
the right angle
and what did you do with that girl, that summer? You couldn't stop kissing her. Always three feet up saying things you couldn't keep and what did it all lead up to? Do you still talk? i saw it all.
Slow-dancing in your kitchen (it used to be me).

I let the phone ring 13 times before I pick up. I'm busy, I say. Always busy, running games in my mind
and I had a great conversation last night with people I've never met and we discussed the opposites of welfare and if I'm a case of it myself and then we all laughed but with a serious tone and had another round on me.

I'm still lonely and it's a glorification of something I'm not finished with. I don't want to be distracted from my work by other people but the absence of it all distracts me from my work and that's why I run towards the city, to get a little glimpse of it.

I never wanted to sell myself short but I got too scared of everything that had to do with anything and now I wish I could have sold myself a little bit. Taken some advice. Listened a bit. Maybe it would have made things easier, for me, a little less heavy. Not light, but less heavy.

I'm passive naiveté and I am walking towards the doom.

The white sheets were reflecting the water outside the window, making ripples on the crystal-clear floor, where we laid, and for a second I wondered how many of my lifetimes I could pay for with one of those lamps, hanging high up on the ceiling. He has too much to know what he has and I believe there could be more value in just a single grain, if you look closely enough, than in a strand of gold.

It was the summer I discovered Kerouac. The endless decadence of free living

and I couldn't help but laugh at it all, the absurdity of my situation, lying on golden sheets reading *The Bhagavad Gita* for the fifth time: non-clinging, non-attachment, preaching freedom, let the clocks ring! but still wanted so badly to press his hands close over my eyes to imagine what it would feel like, to hear something different, something like *hey, why don't you stay for a bit?* just a day or two.
but I never let them. I was up and out before the chance was shot and I preached my detachment as tight as I clung to things and it was the opposition I couldn't clear up.

I wanted to rest so I kept running. Maybe thinking that the faster I ran the sooner I'd arrive, arrive for rest. I wanted company so I kept pushing them away, maybe thinking I could conquer the need for someone or something, and soon I would be free.
I wanted happiness so I clung to objects that could lead me there, one bottle at a time.

Anyway. It's clearer now. It's bright outside. There's an old librarian on the other side of the room putting books in order, a-z, literary history, that's a fine genre. I consume more than I create but I won't feel bad about it because I think I've put out content and emotions and stories that weigh heavy for my age and now I need to put stuff back, to refill those empty holes I walked out with, leaving pieces of myself in every bed I fell asleep on.

I could go on for ages.
I could go on like this forever.

FLICKERS

It was all going too fast. Moments slipped by leaving nothing but flickers and momentary scars and I wanted to stop, right there, on that street, with those people, that taste in my mouth and never lose it. I wanted to feel things for just a little longer, make the spinning stop.

Those were my nights, my mornings, my moments.
They were gone too soon.

Journal III

February 2017

Back to the city....

Jean Jack Rousseau dedicated his last years to recounting and retelling the story of his life. He called it *Confessions*. He wrote down his own life in order to present it in the way he wanted it to be seen and remembered. Was it all the truth? Well, it was his truth. He's a writer.

"No one can write a man's life except himself. His inner mode of being, his true life, is known only to himself; and yet in writing it he disguised it; under the cover of his life's story, he offers an apology; he presents himself as he wants to be seen, not at all as he is."
– Rousseau

He presents himself as he wants to be seen, not at all as he is…

Why this constant urge to explain myself? Why this constant tugging, trying to disguise and conceal, cover up and move on? Why this never-ending yearning for writing down my life and livelihood? Who am I writing for? What do I want you to know? Why do I care?

Maybe I write to you, this book, with the hope that you will find a friend in between these pages. Maybe I write to you, this book, with the hope that you will reach out, tell me "I see you", and I'll say, "I see you too!"

Maybe I want to be gone. Maybe I don't know if I already am, if I'm really here, a part of it all, so I write to make myself come alive, to

be real, to be an actual human being, moving through this world, like everyone else!
Maybe I just don't want this journey to be unseen, unheard of, unknown. Maybe I want someone to understand, me and my ways.

Does anyone really know you? Where are you, except for where you're standing?

Did you change? A little too much to still be you at all, anymore? Are you completely new? Did anyone notice? Do they really know you now? After all these years? You're not the same. You are not the same…

"I see that the people who live most intimately with me don't know me and they attribute most of my actions, whether in good or bad matters, to completely other motives than those which have produced them."
– Rousseau

Maybe I write in order to remember who I've been, who I've become, who I am right now. To observe my life like a researcher and direct my own ways, a little better.
Maybe I write hoping that someone will read it and get to know me through it. Get to know me through my words, my story, as I am now, after all these years.

How I became me? I'm telling you, word by word.

Music on the moon

and we make love like we've never met before
like you've never seen me act up or scream or lose things
like you've never seen me give up, fold it,
get high in the middle of the day
on a Tuesday
because I'm simply done and bored,
unimpressed by it all.
And still you love me like you've never met me before,
like you never came and picked me up
that night
that time
me saying "I'm sorry I'm sorry"
you looking firmly on the road, lips closed tightly
and still you touch me like you don't know about those errors,
those years, the times I did not come home
and I — what am I?

I am the one who will be here and not be here
and you will hear me and then not hear me
and I will come and go as I please
but always come back
saying "I'm sorry I'm sorry I'm sorry"

I might not ever get better.
is there music on the moon?

MY NAME IS ....

Anxious wandering. Never at ease. Just sometimes catching glances of it.
Distance. It's somewhere in the distance.

I find myself sitting on the grass; on the cliff; on his bed
and I'm at ease.

at midnight it starts all over again.

I HAVE NO CARES IN THE WORLD

Youthful days are treasures and it has nothing to do with age.
Still young, I guess, but I remember younger days.
Wide-eyed on every bus to nowhere,
everywhere,
finding melodies and stories,
people to love and lose
and I opened up in different ways.
Shared made-up pasts, shaped and designed to tell and sweep away
like *the poet that I am*
they tell me.
Why tell them about me, when I can tell them about a different me?

... but life grows you ignorant.

I'm walking on an empty country road
somewhere in Sweden
and I have no cares in the world.
I've fought and I've tried. I've seen things, I think to myself
but I'm not happy with what I did or made of myself
and I have no cares in the world.
I spit over my shoulder, get drunk on empty roads
in the middle of the day,
lying on fields in the cold,
cursing how little I grew; how I did not make it.
and I bought new shoes back then, a while ago,
but still wear my old ones.
no money in the bank, no birthday parties to get things wild
for a little while.
I have no cares in the world.

Time taught me to love old things. I'm collecting rings and jewellery and I wear them with tenderness, feeling holy, meditating by the water, in the forest, creating rituals to reach something higher, higher, higher ---
I want to get higher or deeper, somewhere different than this plain, static sense of existence.
Love does the job. travelling too. writing does it. music.
also art, whisky, dark-coloured flowers and watching the landscape change in October. Driving on a small road somewhere in Italy with a beautiful boy and I don't want to be anywhere else in the whole wide world than right there, with him, that very car, smiling.

But I close my eyes for one second and the moment is gone. I'm back to getting high on empty roads somewhere in Sweden and I'm the loneliest girl in the whole damn world and I just want all things beautiful. I just want the music, the literature, the art and the moments of driving in a car with a beautiful boy in Italy.
but here, alone, I have no cares in the world.

I have no cares in the world. I just want it all to be beautiful.

The break-up

"We're breaking up,"
she said, nonchalantly, painting her nails.
"I'm moving soon. A new job. We're both fine."
Except they're not fine.
People are never really
"breaking" up
or
"fine"
just folding it, passively moving on.

So now they're having sex on the fifth floor
casually
breaking it up,
no more feelings,
and next week I'll hear he met another.
Shorter, apparently, younger,
wild, up for fun, not yet worn down by circumstances of adult life
like moving
or money
or moving for money
and I'll see them walking hand in hand
through this town
and people will smile and laugh it off
"this time it's for real!"
and they will make plans and introductions
"this is her!"
he will say
and we will all believe it.

Anyway,
that girl, that thing, will have its way
and I'll hear they folded it last Sunday,
then him preaching words of being happy and free, *finally!*

So now they're having sex on the bathroom floor
and next week I'll see her across the bar with an older man
making moves you only see in movies
I thought
and at midnight they'll walk out hand in hand
and it's all a race to the next starting line.
A merry-go-round, people never cutting deep enough into each other,
or into themselves,
and people don't mean enough for people
like I want them to.
Romances lasting for years
being forgotten in the blink of an eye —

I want love to mean more. It should mean more.
It should cut deeper,
PEOPLE should cut deeper.
They could, if you let them.
I want to believe that things matter,
that people can have an impact.
cut a little deeper.
stay a little longer.
make a little mark,
not to be forgotten.
I don't want her or him or me to be so easily forgotten, and
I want to believe that human interactions can change people,

make someone a little better,
a little lighter,
and it's okay to move on
but not to forget.

It's not okay to forget a person so easily who once took your breath away. Who once made your eyes open wider, made your world a little lighter, a little brighter,
and don't choose to remember all the things you started to complain about at the end. Instead, remember the things you fell in love with, once, back then. The lost little daydreams, the smell in the morning, that ugly oversized hoodie and all the strange little things. How you once used to think them special. Something to miss. Don't throw away things that once mattered to you. Treasure the memories, treasure how that person made you feel, once in your life, like everything was beautiful and nothing could go wrong.

Don't forget someone who once turned your world around.

Memory

It was June and we sat on the stairs of an entrance to a big proud house where formal people worked formal jobs. I loved his guts and he loved his drugs, a dog chasing its tail with no end in sight. The sun was so hot it threw waves on the concrete and I walked barefoot that summer, no shoes needed.

We met by the bar on the beach, the perfect beginning of a sad novel, and I collected stories for future books, I said. Didn't let anything get too close or tight to get to me because I was untouchable. At least so I thought, and it wasn't his company I craved, or anyone else's, it was the fascinating terror of what two people could cause in each other, the storms and marks, and I had a feeling this wouldn't end very well and so naturally I couldn't resist. Too good to pass.

I wrote the novel over and over that summer until I got sick of my own fulfilment of sorrow and threw it in the ocean from the boat back to Sweden and I'm not sure what I wanted to get out of all those nights and weeks with strangers and bottles, but I don't regret it. I don't regret a thing.

Reflection

They say you can trace a person's history, hidden emotions and unhealed scars in their appearance. How you act, how you walk, how you laugh. Do you have a broken heart? It shows. Are you in love? It shows.
They say bad skin reveals stress or anxiety. Do you blink a lot or do you keep a steady gaze during a conversation? Do you talk clearly with a strong support from your stomach, or do you speak quietly and fast, running over your words? Have you ever tried not to eat, just to keep some sort of focus? Sad people either sleep a lot or not at all.

I often wonder what people see when they look at me. What energy do I send out? Do I look happy? Do I look sad? Do I look friendly? Do I look like someone you'd want to hang out with? Do I look like someone you could like?
Do I look insecure, or like I'm strong and sure, a role model to follow? Do I look like someone who threw my fist into a mirror because I simply saw myself in there and couldn't stand the thought of it?

People say there is sadness in my eyes but the sadness sits in my chest so I wonder what it is they see in my eyes.

(A boy told me he likes me better without make-up. What do you reply to that?)

I wonder how my laugh sounds. Do people listen when I speak or do they drift off? If you saw me on the street tomorrow, what would you notice first? Do I look like everyone else? Do I look like someone who figured it out, who grew up, paid for health insurance and got on with it? Or do I look lonely and lost, confused by it all but going on as best I can? Do I take up my space well or am I a ghost walking through the streets?

I wonder about everyone I meet and everyone I've ever met and I wonder how they are, what they're doing, if they're happy, if they're with someone. I hope they are. I hope they're all happy. I hope they're all with someone.
I wonder if they ever think of me, where I ended up, what happened to that girl who was always going somewhere. I wonder if I called now, tonight, just to say "hi," would they want to talk to me? Would they let me in? Forgive and forget? For what...? Not keeping in touch. I could do it now? *hello? i'm sorry. how are you?*

I wonder about my old neighbour in Bristol, the man across the street -- does he still drink his coffee on the porch every morning, even without me waving as I go by? My high school teacher, he was kind to me, telling me I did okay even though I didn't. How are you?

I have this scar on my leg from when I was a kid and did flips on a trampoline but didn't know when to stop, always pushing to the very edge to see how far I could get and I spun over and now there is a story on my body about that very thing and I wonder if people ever notice? My voice gets sore when I drink too much and turns thin when I eat too little and I'm trying to take care of myself, for my voice, the only thing that carries me some days.

Some days I feel healed, does that show? Some days I run and starve and smoke and drink but I feel so happy and I wonder how that makes me look.

Today I woke up, sat in meditation, ate healthy, did my work with a firm mind and I did well. Do I look better now?

Do I look like someone you can trust? You can tell me your secrets. I will listen and understand, I won't tell anyone, I promise. Maybe I can help?
I'm reaching out to people I've left and miss or never knew how to talk to back then—what will they see when they see me now?

Sometimes I feel like a walking representation of loneliness.
Sometimes I feel so strong, like a force of nature.
I've been really happy lately, does that show?

Journal IIII

April 2017

Back to the city....

People my age have stable lives. They went to school, got a job, a house, a car, a marriage… People my age … people my age… People my age grew up and settled in, looking elegant in clean clothes and no split ends,
and people my age go to the hair dresser, invite people over for dinner and drinks, laughing with sophistication, are well-adapted with money in the bank, friends and a clean hall.

I stand on the outside looking in. The kid with a rucksack walking in the snow, peeking through the window. It looks warm in there. Welcoming. A big, clean couch, a thick table carrying coffee-table books and candles just for decoration.

I was going to "make it". I was going to make something of myself. What happened to me?

What happened to me?

Intertwined

People make mistakes and carry them like necklaces too heavy to carry. We're after the chase of it—no one wants *perfect.* No one wants still. We go after it all—the dreams, the money, the things, the ladder—and we end up with it all, bored to death and restless to roam free, make mistakes, mess things up. We find stimulation, novels, drugs, a romance we can't talk about—whatever takes us out of the sterile life we've put ourselves into and we hope it will all go well.
But things can't go well when you don't want them to and your mind is always doing the wrong thing, just for the fun of it, just because what if ... what if ... what if...

Now she's asking for a divorce and wants to keep the house and he doesn't know what beautiful stands for. I keep two hundred metres away watching it all, trying not to make a sound, trying not to make more of a mess than I already have.
But no blame is on me. I'm innocent, they say, though I'm not, and she doesn't have to know, I said, and he did too, but now she does and he throws his arms around not knowing who to look at, where to go, what to keep, what to leave.

I never have anything to lose. People build lives they want to keep and treasure
but I never have anything to lose.

You will go places

My head is never in the right place or state of mind these days, nowadays,
like back then.
I stayed up watching the darkness come and pass and I heard the man in the room next door slam his alarm clock six times before stumbling heavily out and away in suit and tie. I liked the way my fingers ran over those keys. A vague spark from the candle on my desk. I found the desk in a secondhand shop the week I moved there and got it for nothing as long as I could get it home myself. I loved it like the first belonging and piece of furniture I ever had, which it was, and the old dark wood observed me as I went from nothing, back to all and through again that year.
But my mind was sharp. Focused. Not yet blurred out by chemical liquids, numbing sweeter every day, and I had things to say. Anger pumping in my veins, bleeding out like words or sounds or prose on paper and I knew no one would ever care but still I wrote, for my mind was sharp like steel. Back then.

They tell me I have an interesting life. Going places, seeing people, and I shrug my shoulders as I pour another drink,
sitting lonely on my floor in my empty room, another Sunday, in another city, like I've done so many times for so many years and they tell me I'm lucky and should be grateful. And yes, I am grateful. I was grateful walking lonely through a freezing Berlin on Christmas Eve last year
and I was grateful as I lied about my name and job and age to everyone I met and meet
and if you seek the papers where I've been the last years you will find nothing. Or at best, or worst, a spread-out girl leaving small

traces here and there, covering it up with different states of mind
or jobs
or names
and there was a time they said I would go places.
I would go places, they said, once,
way back when.
And this is what I think of as I'm sitting lonely on the train home from another night of beautiful people, welcoming me into their homes with open arms. I played some songs and they hugged me like I've never been hugged before,
by anyone who knows me,
and they told me "thank you" and "I love you"
and hugged me again, like I've never been hugged
by anyone who knows me,
and they were grateful. For me. And so was I. For them.
Human interaction: the most complicated form of happiness I will never figure out.

"You will go places," they told me once, way back when. And if these are the places they predicted for me, I am sorry. I am sorry. I am so very sorry.
I am sorry for the hope you had and the hope I lost and I am sorry for the trust you gave and the trust I lost and I guess that maybe I could reach further and wider, fight harder and better. I thought I would go places too, back then, and maybe I did but I'm not yet sure where they tried to lead me or where I am or where I'm going
and if you have a torch or a fire to burn up the dark
I'll come running like a sinner in the night.
I'll follow whatever direction you give me
for I have none.
I'll follow whatever sign I can find, for

I need a torch in the night.

The stars are too far away
now. The stars are too far away.

Manchester

I left a lover in Manchester
without saying a word
to him, just everyone else,
and I thought I did the right thing. Pulling the stitches without a second thought.
But lately I've had a dream, recurring, him and I, walking.
Always sitting a little too close, always talking a little too slow,
asking me things, never shutting up.
and I think I loved it. the vulgarity of how much he thought he could know
about me
and I let go, go, go,
until words flew free and I spoke without stopping and
did you know this?
and let me tell you about that! and can we go here and do you want to learn this?

But I don't want to try again. I want it like this. Simple. No questions. Silence. Nothing to explain, nothing to understand.

I never closed any doors, just left, and now they all stand open.
The wind is blowing in.

Sometimes.

Sometimes, I go to bed at night, beside someone I love, and I feel this enormous state of pure joy. I feel safe and calm, lucky to get to spend another day filling it with beautiful things and it's all I can ask for.

But then the clock strikes 3 a.m. and BOOM, my eyes are wide open, my heart is pounding like a ticking bomb and there are just too many cars outside. I hear every sound in the whole building and it's too damn dark. I turn around, try to calm my breath, focus on my third eye. It's all okay, it's all okay, you're just tired, go back to sleep. Shhh…
But the feeling won't go away and I sleep in a worried state of unease the rest of the night, with eyes half-open and slightly on the edge.

The morning comes and I try to greet it with tenderness. Be kind to me, okay? Just today. A little softer, just today. I think of all the ways I can spend the hours, to make things nice for myself. All the things I can do, to soften. To bloom. I can go to my favorite coffee shop, read a book in the sun and just be still. And it's warm and summer and think of all the wonderful things ahead! and and and

but the sun is shining way too bright and people are everywhere and I don't know where to go with myself and my room is too messy and plans too many and I can't grasp one at a time and everything flies too fast. My heart keeps beating twice my pace and I'm worried about what?
I.do.not.know

but the anxiety is creeping up and my chest tightens and I lock myself in the bathroom to breathe. I escape wherever whoever I'm with when this happens and I still don't know why it keeps happening but it does and I just get so fucking sad and worried and unstill and I can't stop it.

xx x

It's Monday. It's May. I hurried home like I always do and closed two doors behind me. Made coffee. Meditated. Watered my plants.
People went to their jobs this morning, knowing where to put their bodies on days like this and on days like this I really wish I had somewhere to put my body and focus my mind, because freedom is a privilege that can suffocate you if you don't know how to handle it and on days like this
I don't know how to handle it.

Sometimes we just have to make it through another day.
Sometimes.

"But what did I enjoy when I was alone?
Myself, the whole universe, all that is, all that can be, the entire beauty of the world of sense, the whole imaginable content of the intellectual world: I gathered around me everything that could flatter my heart; my desires were the measure of my pleasures. No! Never have the greatest voluptuaries known such delights, and I have obtained a hundred times more enjoyment from my chimeras than they have from realities."

– Jean Jack Rousseau, *Confessions*

STAY

The years sail on and seasons come and go, and it took me a few hard winters to learn that 'stay' is the saddest word in the English language. There's a reason why I sing it in every song I've ever written and it means more than it says and never sounds the same.
I've said it too many times
and never not only to the person looking me in the eyes
at the time
but to every single soul I've ever left
or been left by
in my whole damned life
and I never learn to say it so that it sounds
quite right
for it's always changing
a little
and I do too
for that's what leaving does to you.
It makes you change with every turn of the back.
Every turn of the season.

Stay; a constellation of *almosts* that never dared to be.

My greatest lines

I wrote my greatest lines at the age of 15,
strumming the only four chords I knew
at the time,
just learning my new guitar
and I remember going to the music store, with a friend, my best friend,
pointing at the black guitar over there, "That one! I want that one!"
And I brought it home and learned those chords and strummed them in all kinds of ways
and I wrote my greatest lines at the age of 15, before the limitations of the real world befell me.

I was free in my innocence, only knowing my own damned states of sorrow, of anger, of eagerness to become something great one day
and I didn't know the world, I only knew my own small town
so I had to make it all up in my head, over and over.
I wrote worlds and wonders, stories and narratives
and I created friends and enemies, lovers and heartbreaks
even though I barely knew the meaning of these words
and that's why
I wrote my greatest lines at the age of 15.

I still didn't know the limitations of the real world, the real meaning behind these real words.
Love was still as magical as in Jane Austen. Heartache was still as real as in Wuthering Heights. Adventure was Kafka on the Shore and life — maybe my life one day — was Jack Kerouac. On The Road and Vagabonding, Rimbaud and Ginsberg.

Yes, this was my world, with no stopping and no *impossibles;* nothing was impossible. Only endless explorations of inner and outer, and there was a time when I got my guitar and learned to strum those chords and sing those notes
that I wrote and wrote, day and night, yes I even forgot to show up at school!
or I went home too early
because I had so many worlds to create and stories to tell, emotions to explore and pains to reveal. So many books to read and songs to hear. Jeff Buckley and Counting Crows, Elliott Smith and Leonard Cohen; and later on, Brand New, Copeland, Ani Difranco!
Yes, there was even a time
at 15 years old
when I thought
to heck with real life. To heck with falling in love out there, or real friends, or losing friends
when I could be happy by myself, here, on my own, writing about it all.
MY REAL. My realness. Safe. True. Maybe?
For real, without knowing the real pain or real hurt. Without having to spend time and effort on that thing out there, "the world". Who needs it?! No, I shall build my own world here, by myself, doing my own thing. With music and art, words and worlds, and I will create my own life. I will build up stories and people, moments and thoughts, and I will learn the tools to make the things I want come alive for real, and then find a few souls out there who might like it too. And I won't need anyone else—won't need anyone to help me, anyone who can hurt me
anyone who can leave me…
disregard me,
anyone…

I won't need anyone…

… I won't need anyone …

I wrote my greatest lines at the age of 15 because I did not know the reality of the words I wrote and that's why it was innocent and effortless and free. So the years went by and I tried to stick to myself, do my thing without any help,
and now I find myself in foreign lands with foreign people not speaking my language,
because I fell for reality and its terrible ways of making loneliness too real to bear.
And then I met a boy who made me weak in the knees, the way I wrote about
at 15
not knowing it could be as real
as this.
and now knowing it's real I'm not sure how to tell. How do you write about something real?
And then there's the real sorrow, the real hurt, the one that shows and bruises
that I did not know about
at 15
because it was all in my head, back then
which is as real as could be
but still.

How do I write about this, now?

I wrote my greatest lines at the age of 15. I have so much left to learn.

Lost ending

It was the night Dave came back from Houston. I was gluing my broken Converse back together when he walked in and I think I must have looked bored, or unimpressed maybe, when I looked up at him.
"Hey what's up, I'm back!"

People come and go all the time, it's ripping me to pieces and I was in a state of simply not caring about anything or anyone other than the very thought of not giving a damn anymore. People always leave, I thought, and I did not want to be excited.
"Cool, how was the big world?" I asked and got back to my shoe work.
"Crazy! Absolutely crazy, let me tell ya. People are greedy as fuck over there. They just want and want and they don't even look you in the eyes when they ask you for something, can you believe that, Charlotte, absolutely crazy! Good to be back."

Greedy people at least want something, I thought, bitter as I was and I guess I was sort of sick of the laziness of people who didn't want anything. The minimalist movement felt cheap and like an excuse to not put the work in. It takes effort to actually make something of impact and I wanted people with unstoppable ambition! I wanted the kind of firm mind you find in athletes, the look in the eyes the second before the runners take off, that will of steel it takes for the swimmers to get back in the lane day after day even though every muscle aches. I was bored of laziness and I was a part of the problem but I was just waiting it out, I thought. In the spring I would take off. I was just sharpening my sword.

I always pictured it a grand thing, the moment I would take off. Someone waving long after I was out of sight and some tune playing soft from somewhere I couldn't see. I pictured it a clear line, some sort of sharp edge between before and after. But there is no such thing. You can take a U-turn where you're walking on the pavement but people are just on their own ways home, and now you're in their way. You keep walking against the tide and you think you're doing something great but really you're just pissing people off and when you finally get out on the open field where no directions exist, you find yourself lonely, not free, just a big, vast lonely world that surrounds you and you can go anywhere you please but suddenly you don't want to go anywhere at all. You just want to go home. Back to your people. Back to your bed. To your things and the warmth and a nice shower and something to drink.

There is no happy ending to this story. Maybe one day I'll write it.

Growing up is a wonderful thing to do

Journal V

May 2017

Back to the city....

I am entering a new phase. I am done with my childish sorrow. I no longer want to vagabond my way through life, a little to the right, feeling left behind. I want to become a person of warmth and integrity. I want to feel certain and at peace, knowing my own worth and ways, and I want to create my own self and my own life and I no longer want to feel left behind.

Maybe I can grow into someone I will be proud to be.

It's time to grow into someone I'm proud to be.

I don't want to be an author

What am I trying to be?
What am I creating of myself?

I don't want to be an author.
I don't want to be a songwriter.

I don't want to be a prose writer, a columnist, a poet. I don't want to be a Twitter phenomenon, an eternal wanderer, a runner, an actress. I am not a singer and I am not a publisher.
I am the sum of all these things, expanded and built upon, creating something unique that I—and only I—can carry, and I am not a label. I am not a brand.

I am not something you can touch or dress up, replicate or reproduce
and I am nothing special. In the literal sense, for this speaks for all of us—or rather, we who dare to throw off the labels, get off the paved road to a finished title and instead create our own undefinable titles.
I am the sum of everything I do and learn and read and hear
and all these things become my paint; my melodies; my pencils. The decorations I will use to build my very own self. To look and feel and talk like I want to, and it might sound grand and naive, but I am the creator of my very own self and I intend to treat me like my greatest masterpiece. There are things and creations that no one can ever touch, only feel, hear and remember, and I believe that impact is bigger than any label or name anyone can ever give me. I must believe that what I create is bigger than myself. That I—Charlotte Eriksson—can go under the surface and not be remembered by

name, not recognised by face, but what I manage to create and build, learn and acknowledge … will be remembered. Forever. Eternally. Internally, be of impact, for someone.
I want no name. I want no fame.
I want impact.

I am a worried person with a stressed-out soul, living a simple life with no capital. I am gathering knowledge in every corner I can with the abilities I have. I'm reading philosophy, politics, history and fiction. Greek tragedies and the arctic waste. I'm studying psychology, economics, plant-based nutrition and I'm writing essays and manifestos, chasing bigger names with bigger frames, to ask a question or two, and I am learning to lead.
I am reading to take the lead.
Lead who? Myself. My own life. My own future. I'm not chasing you, or them, or anyone else; I am chasing me.

For I have nothing to lean on, nowhere to call my home and there is nowhere I will go for Christmas to rest my head and touch familiar walls. I have no degree to show on paper or employment to take care of my health or the reassurance that I can pay my rent. And I have no right to complain because this is the road I chose and I built it myself, not really knowing where I wanted it to lead, but I have hope in all things ahead and behind and I am learning to let myself go. Forget my own ego and believe that what I am doing is grander than my own self.

I believe … that you must collect and pursue all your passions. Let your desires lead you to foreign territories. And your path might look scattered for now, like you have no direction or clear aim, but I believe that one day, all these ideas and spread-out skills will combine and create a creation of impact, a combined masterpiece of everything you found to love, and that will be your legacy.

Don't limit yourself: expand yourself. Don't just be an artist … be everything you could ever be.

I'm not exactly sure where all this will lead me, but I know it's leading me somewhere. My only task it to embrace everything as if it was laid out before me, as if I was destined to stand in front of every situation I will ever face, and my task is to walk this Earth with ease and grace, certain of my place. My experiences will sculpt and shape me into something unique and of importance, and though it's months of cold and now it's getting dark before it's getting late, I must believe that there will be a day when the sun wakes up before I do, again. When the grass grows green and the soil will feed the marrow once more, and just like this, or that, I must believe that I am building right now, here, doing this. And it will one day bloom like the most wonderful flower, growing stronger underneath that soil.

I must believe in my own growth, and trust the pace of nature.

As long as I am moving I am right on the path I made.

Memory

That was the summer I kept my eyes on him through the window as the train kept leaving faster and faster, the silhouette of him turning vaguer and vaguer. I held my eyes on him without blinking, scared I would lose sight. That was the summer I said goodbye to people and places through train windows. Going faster, going nowhere, and that was the summer I started over, over and over again.

That was the summer I did not know how to say my name without flicking my eyes because I couldn't live up to the name I was known as, and that was the summer I got a new one.

Journal VI

July 2017

Growing up is a wonderful thing to do

I've been thinking a lot about the pretty awkward and hard, but necessary transition from being a young artist trying to figure things out, to being a woman of artistic confidence. A woman owning her knowledge, skills and place as a creative person. For a long time I felt very behind, not at all like an adult with any right to call myself this or that. I was an aspiring songwriter, an aspiring author. I mumbled my introductions, didn't know what I actually wanted to say I did or was and I was just a kid, too young for any responsibility.
But now I've been walking the very same roads back and forth and I walk them differently. So I've been trying out some new things, just for myself, to see if it feels good. New sounds, new people, new clothes, new ways of talking. And as you change there are people who in an instant screams "that's not like you!" and I keep quiet thinking… not like me… what me? Eighteen-year-old me? No, how I speak today is definitely not like eighteen-year-old me, because I'm twenty-six and I hope to god I don't speak and look and think like I did when I was eighteen. I encourage growth and development and I wish to grab a bit of it every single day.

The truth is, twenty-year-old Charlotte who slept at airports and train stations, busked to afford some coffee and wrote novels about being lost, was a beautiful version to be, at twenty, but I don't want that to be who I am when I'm thirty. So I've spent a lot of time thinking about who I aspire to be. What I aspire to stand for. What I want people to feel and know and think when they hear my name.
"Charlotte Eriksson, thirty, songwriter & author."

That feels good, but what do I want that to mean? What do I want that to stand for?

I want to grow into a woman of integrity and intelligence. I want to be known for my brevity, for independence, for making things happen. I want to be known as someone humble, kind, warm and awake. Someone you can talk to, who will listen and care. But I also want to have respect from myself. I want to have high standards and reach for the best. I want to create things of importance, that will be received with the same amount of respect it was created with. I want to work with diligence and quality. Put my growth as an artist and writer above all else and never belittle my ability to create something of value. Something that has a place in the world. I want to be given the space and freedom to explore and delve deeper than what's expected of me. I want to never disappoint, myself or anyone else, but I want to not be afraid of pushing the boundaries a little. Step a little closer to the edge, a little to the left. With my words and with my voice. With pictures and visuals, dare to look as I feel and own it without apologising and I want to be so sharp and authentic that no one can ever doubt what I'm about. I no longer want to explain myself. I want my work to be clear enough to do the talking.

I'm not there yet, but I strive to be constantly creating myself, and this is important to me. I want to grow into a woman of integrity, strength and warmth, and the work towards that person starts now. Maybe before I'm ready, but if I don't start aiming towards this picture now, I will fall behind my own vision. I will fall short for the comfort of being young and lazy, painting a little out of the line and find excuses for it.
I don't think you should be scared of growing up or of showing your maturity. I am no longer a lost kid and I don't want to act like

one. I want to own my confidence and my role in this society and I want to be as respected as any other.

I spent so many years breaking mirrors because I could not stand the thought of myself in this body. But I am not fighting myself anymore. I know I can do things, if I put the effort in, just like everyone else.

Humbly but bravely.

Love with wholeness

I want to learn how to love with wholeness. Give myself to experiences so fully that I forget about how people will perceive it, or how other people see me, or who I am or used to be.

I want to meet new people and ask one question that will lead them into new patterns of talking and I want to learn how to listen. How to hear and see and understand in a way that makes them feel safe, and home, and comfortable enough to tell me more even though I don't ask for it.
I want to stop letting my fear of being seen as someone I'm not stop me from doing things I don't usually do,
and I want to learn how to drive on empty roads with nowhere to go and no time in mind,
and I want to know what it feels like to fall exhausted down on the floor late at night thinking *what a hell of a ride*,
and I want to know what it feels like to hold someone's hand without wanting more than just that.

I don't want to live in my head anymore for I am here right now and that is beautiful and important and I want to learn how to not take it for granted.
I want to feel fully alive. Alive and aware of everything right here right now and not wish for more than just what is.

I want to learn how to love with wholeness. Grasp it completely, like the grandest full moon in the middle of the sky, and not wish for it to lead to anything more or less than just that.
I want to be fully aware of everything I have. Here. Now. Today. Tonight.

Anxiety

Yesterday it was sunny outside. The sky was blue and people were lying under blooming cherry trees in the park. It was Friday, so records were released that people have been working on for years. Friends around me find success and level up, do fancy photo shoots and get featured on big white movie screens. There were parties and lovers, hand in hand, laughing perfectly loud,
but I walked numb through the park, round and round,
40 times for 4 hours,
just wanting to make it through the day.

There's a weight that inhabits my chest sometimes. Like a lock in my throat, making it hard to breathe. A little less air got through
and the sky was so blue I couldn't look at it because it made me sad, swelling tears in my eyes, dripping quietly on the floor as I got on with my day. I tried to keep my focus, ticked off the to-do list, did my chores. Packed orders, wrote emails, paid bills and rewrote stories,
but the panic kept growing, exploding in my chest. Tears falling on the desk
tick tick tick
me not making a sound
and some days I just don't know what to do. Where to go or who to see and I try to be gentle, soft and kind,
but anxiety eats you up and I just want to be fine.
This is not beautiful. This is not useful. You cannot do anything with it and it tries to control you, throw you off your balance and lovely ways.
But you must not let it.

I cleaned up. Took myself for a walk. Tried to keep my eyes on the sky. Stayed away from the alcohol, stayed away from the destructive tools we learn to use.
The smoking and the starving, the running, the madness,
thinking it will help when it only feeds the fire
and I don't want to hurt myself anymore.

I made it through and today I woke up, lighter and proud because I'm still here. There are flowers growing outside my window. The coffee is warm, the air is pure. I have books to read and songs to sing, people around that I like and can laugh with,
and it's spring again.
It will always be spring again.
There will always be a new day.

If you're like me, just trying to make it through the day, I'm here to show you that you can.
You will always be okay.
You will bloom again.

Maybe it's never too late to start over?

I'm going back to places I left. I reach out to people I once knew, but forgot to call or keep in touch with and now I need it. I was a half-finished person, a blurry draft someone forgot to complete and I wanted to create myself before I had people close to me again. I no longer wanted to feel shame or embarrassment over my own persona, so I left and did not keep in touch. I cut all the connections and tried to build up and start anew.

But life on the road is a lonely one. Everyone you meet is going somewhere, or you are — one of you will leave. I kept leaving. Kept packing up and packing out and making everything lighter the best I could and now I find myself lonely and adult, ready for a life I once had but didn't know how to take care of.

If I could go back and do things again I would treasure more things, not just leave and let them hang. I would keep in touch. I would say *I'm sorry.* I would go to the party and stay the night. I would pick up the phone when my friend needed me even though I was busy because one day I would need her, but I did not pick up back then. She called someone else.

I would do my homework as well as possible because I didn't know then that, more than skills in mathematics and history, it was a practice of character: to do all things well, no matter what, and keep disciplined. I would nourish my talents and take them seriously, repeat and stay focused. I wouldn't shrink myself, act up or go wild at fifteen years old because I was scared, and sad, just confused by it all.

But there is no going back and there is no doing over. There is only this. The road I paved and walked and all I can do is make things right now, do better, work with what's left.
So I go back to places and people, cleaning up best I can. Correcting and finishing, like I never learned how to do, only leave and start anew, and I am tired of running because of shame.
I write short letters, never knowing how to start. Do I say I'm sorry? For what? Do I tell about my journeys? Do I ask about theirs? Do they want to know? Do they even remember me? Do I introduce myself, again? Am I all gone or still there? How much can I ask? How late is too late?
I go back to projects, and jobs, songs and tasks. I clean up, erase, make it better, make it right.

I cleaned out my closet and bought books on social skills because the other day I met a woman my age but I felt like fifty years younger. She spoke with clarity and comfort, about all things worldly, and I found myself listening like never before and I want to learn how to do the same. I no longer want to flick my eyes and speak under my breath, mumbling because of shame or insecurities from ten years ago that are still bugging me. I wanted to ask her so many things but also just stand there, next to her, because it made me feel calm, and I want to grow the same. Calm and sure, just certain of it all.

I would like to treasure a little more. Treasure moments and nights, people and feelings. I wouldn't rush so much, wouldn't try to just get it over with. I would take it all in and say "I love you" more. Say, "Call me if you need me", say, "You can visit any time".

But now I work with what I've got. I go back and keep in touch.
Maybe it's never too late to start over?
Maybe it's never too late to get it right.

Move with grace

They all ask me:
What do you want to do with your life, Charlotte?
What do you want to be?
Where do you want to live?

I tilt my head to the other side, letting my eyes wander deep into theirs. I notice a soft touch of wind on my chin, grabbing hold of my hair. The sky is full of clouds, shifting and reshaping, making space to fill it up again.

What do you want to do with your life, Charlotte? Where do you want to live?

I've lived half my life in constant restriction. Restricting my body from growing, blooming, shaping, shifting. Restricting my heart from loving too much, feeling too much, hurting too deeply. I lived half my life restricting my surroundings, or, restricted by my surroundings. *Don't go too far, don't move too far, don't leave the ground.*

But my body is a temple and I was not born to live in chains. I stand on a mountain, in a forest, by the water, and I feel free. I feel free to breathe and move, flex and shape
and I let my chest open and close.
I let my eyes go and breath go and I feel the wind moving me, from within, and I let go.

What do you want to do with your life, Charlotte?

I want to move with no restrictions. I want to grow and flex and reshape, a little every day, and I want to listen to natural sounds, playing melodies in the air, and I want to close my eyes, believe in what I feel and I want to let this inner melody guide me. Move me.

It's like a melody moving me from the inside and when I listen closely enough, I can hear it.

I want to live here, in this, in the guiding of my own inner rhythm and I want to be this: a force of nature, moving wherever it feels right, and I want my life to be this: a temple of strength and grace, a torch in the night, a sacred space of healing.

Close your eyes.
Place your hand on your heart.
Do you hear it?
What about now?

That's your rhythm. Move with that.

PART TWO

Humbly But Bravely

INTRO PART TWO

Somewhere far up north ...

The air is crisp and pure as it only is a few weeks every year, high up, on certain mornings. I've spent months waking up by fabricated alarm sounds and nothing but thunder in my chest, lying still with my eyes closed for as long as I can. But today my eyes shot wide open with no effort. I smiled, without thinking, without trying. I've read that spiritual gurus in India believe that busy people in the West only breathe in and out halfway throughout their lives—we only use 50% of our lungs and leave toxic air in there because we never fully breathe out, and never fully breathe in, to fill our lungs with fresh oxygen. We breathe in the pace of our hectic lives and so the other half of our lungs is filled with old air without life force. I sit up and take five deep breaths, in—out—swimming through the air and the sun is warming up my bones, a warmth I only felt once or twice maybe, being happy for reasons I can't recall.

I've sought the city—the busy life—because I wanted something. I wanted a name, a chance, a shot at becoming something more than just another soul who kept on walking and I wanted it all. The glory, the rapport. But I kept chasing and I still want things. There are so many songs and dreams in my head and I thought I would grow out of this—feeling overwhelmed by the mere thought of life. But I haven't. Not yet. I still panic as soon as I get important letters from a society that I can't seem to grasp. I regret things I said to lost friends years ago and I daydream about going back to cities and nights, to make it right. Clean up my past and story and just get it right.
I remember my teenage years as a blurry haze and it makes me angry. I wasted it. So many chances, and I see now how it all comes back around. If I had done that differently this would have happened and

if I could have stayed with that person this wouldn't have happened and if I had gone right instead of left I wouldn't have ended up in that place, that night, and I just can't move on. I can't settle in. I can't settle in with this life and body and I don't want to waste it.

It's 6 a.m. and I'm sitting high up on a mountain somewhere in the north of Sweden. It's August and the sun is out 23 hours every day here. So I slept outside under a bare sky, and usually it would frighten me these days, the constant threat of all things worldly. The girl who spent her youth sleeping at airports, train stations, on floors and couches, with no fear other than not succeeding—is now afraid of exactly everything. I'm afraid of it all. Walking alone at night, flying, driving, big crowds, meeting new people, politics, love, trying and failing and missing every chance I might get and I don't know when this all started but somewhere along the way the fearless youth directed her eyes toward the ground and started mumbling sorries and apologies. For what? Who knows. Everything? I'm sorry for things I say and don't say, things I do and don't do. I'm sorry for not living vaster and better, taking more space, taking less space. Sorry to myself and all around and damn it! I have things to change and things to learn, so I left the city and went north. What I'm looking for I don't know, but at least I can breathe here and that makes me calm. I breathe, in, out, sitting cross-legged on the ground. The sun is rising over the treetops and I have absolutely no plan for anything, towards nowhere. Freedom is a privilege I was given way too early, and it's time I learn how to handle it.

I'm twenty-six. What does that make me? My friends are split into two camps: the freewheelers who are still travelling Australia on no budget, no job, no education, and couldn't be happier—and the responsible ones. The ones who went to school, got a job, moved to

Stockholm, got an apartment; a partner; a car; a kid. And what am I? I'm forever stuck in a nonexistent place where no time passes and I do so much and learn so much but I don't grow. I'm still teenage me wanting more. Wanting less. Wanting anything and everything and I think I should grow up now. Grow out of childish anxiety and sorrows for all things past and everyone has moved on from schools and neighbourhoods and I moved first and swore the loudest on never coming back but now I dream about all things past. Going back. How do you transition from being a lost teenager, to one of those calm and serene souls of integrity and certainty? Because that's what I must do, now, soon. Do others feel left behind too, or is it just me? Like the train left with everyone on it and I'm still standing on the platform trying to decide if I should watch the sky for another hour or go change my ticket. Maybe sometimes you need to just close your eyes and jump on the train without feeling ready, and grow your steady breath on the way. I think sometimes you don't know how much you're capable of until you're forced to grow into it.

So, I'm here to create myself. Shed my own behaviour and thoughts like a snake and carefully build a new pattern. Because I'm not happy as me, yet, still. And I don't want to meet the world until I am. Maybe I'm far away from it, but ageing scares me. It matters to me, to feel it, to meet each age like someone I would want to be at that age of my life because … it simply matters to me. I'm an artist and I want to create myself. Like every song I've ever written, crafted carefully with heart and soul but somehow I forgot to care about my very own self in the same way, so my songs are strong but I am not. I take pride in my songs, but in me … I don't.
I don't want to turn thirty and still feel like eighteen, so I am starting now, to create the thirty-year-old me I'd like to be in four years.

Maybe I can grow into her and finally feel like I've caught up with it all. I want to be steady. Assured. Strong. I want to walk with grace and integrity, a certainty about where I'm going and what I want, so strong that no one can doubt it and I want to meet everyone with love and clarity. I want people to feel calm when they're around me. Calm and inspired because life is an adventure and everything will be fine. I want to be a bringer of peace and healing. But also hard work. I believe in it—work, that is. I believe in throwing yourself into that thing you've decided to be and pursue it, and I believe in never backing down. Be so good they can't ignore you. Be good for yourself. Because it's bigger than you. Because this is what you came here to do and you never have to question it once you've made up your mind.

I want to be a songwriter. I want to be a friend. I want to be a writer and author, creator of all things lovely, pure, dark and mystical and I want to be the one who dares to put words on things that might hurt. Things that might make people flicker their eyes in discomfort, but I want to be the one with a steady gaze, saying: this is what I feel and have experienced and I'm not alone, neither are you. Now let's acknowledge it.

Why are people so ashamed of certain feelings? Why are people so ashamed of certain experiences? The things we struggle with? Weaknesses. The nights of tired surrender. When we lose control, fall from grace, moments of self-deception. So we said something stupid or stumbled in the dark. We're universal copies, with the same brains and lives and we're all going through the same journey of growing from kids to teenagers to young adults to somewhat adult—to maybe a little calmer, to even more calm, and some lose their ways here but I want to speak up about it and hear that we're all on the same journey. We're all on the same road but it feels like everyone's ashamed of walking this road so everyone's looking down, trying not to be seen, pretending their feet are steady and not stumbling.

I want the women and men before me to throw a glance over their shoulder and see me down there, beneath the hill, trying to figure out how to start climbing and how they made it, and I want them to simply give me a reassuring smile and say: "Charlotte, you've done great. Just start climbing but do it on the left path because I took the right one and it was the harder one, so now I'm advising you to go left. Come, follow me, but enjoy the way up for you'll never walk it again and the view is quite breathtaking."
I want someone before me to reach out a hand, acknowledge the climb I'm trying to make and just say: "Come, follow me."

Where are our heroes? Where are our role models? Why are we leaving youth behind and laughing at the ones who are still there? Why not help each other out instead? with a little grace. with a little compassion. Love for all and everyone around because we're all stumbling or succeeding back and forth, every day, and I want more community. I want helpers and guidance. Am I helping someone? I don't know, but since the tender age of eighteen I have written down my stories and experiences of love and loss and youth, just so these stories can exist in the world. For someone out there to find and read and feel a voice in my words saying, "I've been there, I've done this, you can too: come, follow me."
Have you ever lost something by teaching what you know, and learning what you don't know? Have you ever lost something by helping someone in need, or letting someone help you while in need? Have you lost something by loving? In comparison, how much have you lost by meeting someone with ignorance and hate?

Love. I will choose love. And I'm scared and shy, of everyone and everything, to make a fool of myself; to be laughed at; to not be what people would like me to be. But I will choose love because that's the sort of person I want to be.

I want to take on the journey of creating myself, and I want to be the person who refused to settle. I want to be the sort of person who keeps questioning, learning, building, creating—so that's what I'm going to do. I want to be a person who never gives up. Who made up her mind about something and followed through—so that's what I'm going to do. You have to act as the person you desire to be.

So I went north, for I have things to figure out and clear up, and I am not the first one to do this climb and not the last one who will. I have searched every shelf of every library I've ever been to, to read about someone else's journey of growing into her skin—but in vain. So now I'm writing the story I wanted to read but could not find, because I want it to exist in the world. Because I believe it should exist in the world. Because I hope the next lost soul who's at the beginning of this hill finds it, and can hear me, reaching out a hand saying: "You're doing just fine. Come, follow me."
We must create the world we want to live in.

Twenty-six. Lost. Somewhere far up north. Who can I be here?

I'm trying, as I always will

I get so goddamn lonely and sad and filled with regrets some days. It overwhelms me as I'm sitting on the bus, watching the golden leaves from a window; a sudden burst of realisation in the middle of the night. I can't help it and I can't stop it. I'm alone as I've always been and sometimes it hurts.

But I'm learning to breathe deeply through it and keep walking. I'm learning to make things nice for myself. To comfort my own heart when I wake up feeling sad. To find small bits of friendship in a crowd full of strangers. To find small bits of joy in a blue sky, from a trip somewhere not so far away. A long walk on an early morning in December, or a handwritten letter to an old friend with nothing but "I thought of you. I hope you're well."

No one will come and save you. No one will come riding on a white horse and take all your worries away. You have to save yourself, little by little, day by day. Build yourself a home. Nurture your body. Find something to work on. Something that makes you excited, something you want to learn. Get yourself some books and learn them by heart. Get to know the author, where he grew up, what books he read himself. Take yourself out for dinner. Dress up for no one but you and simply feel nice. It's a lovely feeling, to feel pretty. You don't need anyone to confirm it.

I get so goddamn lonely and sad and filled with regrets some days, but I'm learning to breathe deep through it and keep walking. I'm learning to make things nice for myself. Slowly building myself a home with things I like. Colours that calm me down, a plan to follow when things turn dark. A few people I try to treat right, even though I don't sometimes, but it's my intention to do so. I'm learning.

I’m learning to make things nice for myself. I’m learning to save myself.

I’m trying, as I always will.

Places of home

I go back to places I've been to. Corners of my heart where I collect moments of home.

Beautiful places are not just a joy for the moment, while you're there. They will become homes for you, spaces of solace and comfort, where you can close your eyes and go to.
In the middle of the chaos, in the middle of the cold. In the middle of the world spinning way too fast,
and if you place your hand above your heart you will feel it there. The stillness. Maybe the laughs from the boys playing football close by. Maybe a boat far out at sea. You'll hear the waves, making their ways, and a soft breeze. You'll feel the energy spread in your chest and out in your veins and your breathing will get deeper, quieter, softer.

Now open your eyes. Those places you miss, those moments you miss; you own them. They're yours, within you. Nothing you experience will ever go away. It belongs to you now. Just feel. Don't be afraid to feel.

I go back to places I've been to. Corners of my heart where I collect moments of home.

Everything Changed When I Forgave Myself

I have crooked teeth. I was born with strange toes and sometimes my heart speeds up. I'm not good with people, always keeping to myself, and I have two brothers I don't even know.
But I'm trying to smile even though my teeth don't look like a toothpaste commercial. I'm walking bare-foot, thinking "who decided how toes are supposed to look?" and I'm trying not to wear oversized clothes just to hide my body. I still keep to myself a lot but sometimes I try to show up and reach out, and sometimes that's all it takes.
I'm trying to both love myself and grow myself.

Everything changed when I learned to honour my body instead of fighting it. When I learned to take care of it, like a precious castle to protect this weary heart. To stop harming it, punishing it for looking like this or that, feeling like this or that. I don't look like they all told me I had to, but I'm healthy and strong and vital. That is enough.

Everything changed when I forgave myself.
I never got a record deal. I never found a manager who believed in what I did. I never got to tour in a bus, with a band, in front of big crowds, and I never got to do all those things I fought all my life for, for so long.
But I started my own record label and built my own deal. I learned to manage myself and embarked on my own tour. With friends as a band and believers as a crowd.
I carved my own path.
Everything changed when I switched from saying "I have to do this" to "I GET to do this". When I started viewing my music as a way to serve instead of building for my own profit. When I tried to meet

people with an open heart and a will to love them instead of guarding my own history of solitude and brokenness.

Dedication. Giving. Loving.
That is the goal.

Everything changed when I forgave myself for all the things I couldn't be.
I'm not famous, successful, rich or popular. I don't have a large group of friends, a big house or academic qualifications to get me a job: heck I never even had a job!
But I get to do me. Full out. Peacefully. With no one telling me to go there or do that, be this or sign here. I get to explore every corner of my own personality, on my own terms. Every passion, every talent, and follow wherever it might lead me.

I'm not everything I want to be, but I'm more than I was, and I'm still learning.

I'm happy, just sitting here. Knowing I have a few friends. Knowing I have a dream to work on. Knowing I have somewhere to go if it starts raining. A pillow to rest my head on. Someone to call when I get lonely. Nature to walk in, pure air, early mornings, seasons and weather. This is enough. This is more than enough.
And most of all, I am enough.

Everything changed when I forgave myself.

I have everything to make me glad I'm alive

It's important to contradict yourself a little. To not settle into a sort of sense-making, fitting the mould, never making heads turn. Get yourself a little shook up. Open your eyes and say, "What did I just do? What's gonna happen now?"

Disturb the structures. Do what people thought you'd never do and smile when they can't believe it.
Jump on that train, quit your job, go to Berlin and get gone in a dark nightclub. Fall in love with someone different and learn the sweet sound of lonely roads, walking home with no hurry, just in time for the sunrise. Sell your closet, make some money and spend it on something useless.
Do it all over again and don't think twice about it.

Ah, the glorious pursuit of life … it's never-ending!

Journal VII

October 2017

Back to the city....

I'm catching glimpses of it. A firm state of mind. A constant stream of well-being rushing through me, from the sky through my being to the ground, where I stand, feeling connected. I'm catching glimpses of myself, slowly. That 'me' I'm trying to create, getting clearer and closer every day. She's standing somewhere—everywhere—looking sure, calm and graceful. Strong.

I reach moments when it all aligns. I created this life with my own hands, carefully collecting passions and skills, people and roads, and I made it my own. I wrote it down and sang it out and I catch glimpses of a woman with two feet on the ground but head in the clouds, not feeling the need to explain herself: her actions say it all. And people feel safe and inspired, just being around her, and her word is *belonging.*

Short moments of complete clarity when I'm not scared. Moments when I feel strong enough to know that the universe has my back, it's on my side.

I'm catching glimpses of it. They're lasting longer each time.

Hope

I have hope
in who I am becoming.

I have belief in every scar and disgraceful word
I have ever spoken
or been told
because they are still teaching me.
I have hope in who I am becoming.

They say it takes 756 days to run to someone you love
and they also say that the only romance worth fighting for
is the one with yourself,
and I know by now
that they say a lot of things,
people talking everywhere
all the time
without saying a word.
But if it took me all those years to learn myself,
or teach myself
how to look into the mirror
without breaking it,
I know for a fact that it was a fight worth fighting.

I stood up for my own head and so did my heart
and we are coming to terms with ourselves.
Shaking hands
saying, "Let's make this work,
for we have places to go
and people to see,

and we will need each other."
So I have hope
in who I am becoming.

I have hope in who I am becoming.

No witness but the moon

Where would you go if you could go anywhere? Where do you go when the whole world is yours to find and explore, nothing to see but everything? Where do you start? Which road do you walk first?

What would you do if you could do anything and no one would ever know about it? Who would you want to be if no one would see who you've become? What goals would you want to fight for, if the only person who would know about your achievements would be you?

London at midnight

I'm sitting in the taxi
at midnight
raving through London streets.
Youths and lonesomes are running this place.
September. End of summer—new beginnings,
and I'm happy for the short moments of clarity,
sitting in a taxi at midnight
feeling free, for once.
Burdens pushed away and I could go anywhere I want from here.
No one would miss me.

The driver asked how my night was and I asked him back and he
looked at me and said
"My night is always good," and I smiled, like you do.

I get books as gifts from people now
because they know I treasure them more than any other material
belonging
I could be given
and I read them like teachers, like words from the Lord.

There is action outside that door, kid.
There are people falling in love and getting sick and running away
and there are parties on a moonlit beach somewhere in Australia
and in Ireland an old folksinger is singing poetry you won't be able
to hear somewhere else,
and in Germany there's a boy busking with a beat-up guitar and a
worried mom at home,
and you could be one of them.

One of them doing things, finding voices, creating things
and you could be one of them.

Leave that room, kid. Shut the screen off. Take your dirty shoes, not the pretty ones, and go out to feel the wind. Touch water. Touch earth. Touch wood, touch skin, touch everything you can touch and memorise everything because that's all you will live off in the end, and that's all you will need.

I give the taxi driver a bigger tip than I really can because it feels right to do so on this special night,
and I walk home smiling, knowing the world will still be here when I wake up.

Journal VIII

January 2018

Back to the city....

I was sitting watching the rain this morning, having a coffee in my usual way, and it hit me that I no longer feel left behind. I have worked my way back. I no longer feel childish, catching up, not understanding. I feel … ready. In perfect harmony with my time and age and year and pace and I feel … worked out. Shaped … carefully drawn and created, pieced together and now after all those years: Strong. Assured. Adult? slowly. I'm getting there, I really am.

I found a way. I survived.

I expected it to be a terrible fall down into the abyss, the moment I realised I'd grown up. But instead, I'm having these pure moments of solace and peacefulness. A calm sense of wonder for how I somehow made it from there … to here. I made it. Both literally and metaphorically, because I would never consider myself successful but still I sat in that chair this morning feeling … just, successful.

How does one know you've "made it"?
You no longer feel like you have anything to prove to anyone. You have no regrets or resentments from the past, anger that you're working from. No people you want revenge on or songs you want to sing in order to finally speak your mind.
Instead, you work from a place of wanting to do the work only, without any attachment to the outcome. Sure, it would be nice with a song being spread far and wide and a book picked up by literary greats, but my pleasure lies in the work itself, crafting my crafts. The

studying, collecting knowledge about subjects and themes and people and places. Art, history, politics, economics, psychology, philosophy! It all interests me! It gives me awe and wonder for how much there is to learn and create and I can't wait to sit down and make something. For myself—of myself!
The pleasure lies in the work and my work does not finish until it has reached someone out there. One soul, two souls, maybe three? How great!

Great growth comes from loneliness. You have time to develop, dwell in your own mind and go a bit mad. All the great people are a bit mad. That's good to remember. Don't escape it.
Great growth comes from time spent in foreign lands, watching foreign people with foreign cultures. It makes you forget about your own land and race and town for a while.
Great growth also comes from rooting yourself into one place from time to time. Unpack your bags, get a nice bed, a bookshelf, some friends. Learn to show up, keep in touch, stick around.

Growth comes in all sorts of forms and shapes, everywhere at all times, and it's yours to take and consume. Do what ought to be done. Here and now, to get you somewhere—anywhere.

I feel a new era coming in, standing on the shore, waiting for it to slowly greet me.

The Flow of Life

It's the constant flow of life that keeps me going. The way it always pulls me back. As long as I keep doing the only thing it tells me to, which is, in fact, to simply keep going.

I keep the dawn company as the sky is turned into a painting of pink and crisp air, sitting cross-legged on the ground, closed eyes, no sound. It takes a lot, sometimes, to stand the lack of everything else but the simple act of breathing. Inhale, exhale, "I am I am I am".
As long as I do my part, my heart will do its part.

So it's the constant flow of life that keeps me going.
For I've been down in the darkest wells too many times and I've bought tickets back home, put up ads for my guitar and few belongings because I've been done. Done with myself and them and all the rest and I've been too ashamed to leave my room, too scared to say yes and too damn stubborn to reach for those hands willing to help me up,
but there is something about the constant flow of life that keeps me going. *As long as I do my part, my heart will keep doing its part.*

I was born in the cold, with the winds and the snow, and a Winter Girl I've always been, and always will be, for it's in my blood, you see. But there is something about the way my mind switches, a little more each day, nowadays, and I don't know if it's just the time of year or the time of month that makes it clear.
Or the way he says my name,
or the way I like his ways.
How he takes his place
in this world,

or the way he simply is.
Or maybe it's just the summer deceiving my soul, but still I am surprised when I catch myself making gestures to the moon, saying "hi" and "goodnight".
My own ways. The contradiction I never figured out.

I'd like to give the credentials to my friends that they deserve, for I was done and numb and nowhere to be found. Unwilling to go or stay or anything else and I was done. It was another long winter and my bags still unpacked, both for the lack of travel and for the lack of coming home, so I slept on the floor with three layers of clothes, dry and cold as stone.

People are everywhere and most of the time in my way, blurring my view, but still they are as rare as simple mornings, for I've never been someone to join in or simply go along.
People are rare for people like me, for I tend to stick to myself when the day comes to its end and I have my habits and routines. Hidden well behind my shell and I am constantly torn between the will to be seen and still
hidden so goddamn well:
a contradiction I never figured out.
So when someone gets close enough to see and hear and simply not walk right through me, it affects my very self and all my ways,
for people are rare
for people like me
and I'm tired of always running.
And still,
I just simply like his ways.
How he says my name
and the place he takes

and all
that he is
in and of himself.

Anyway, it's the constant flow of life that keep me going, the way it always pulls me back, when I tell myself I'm done and finished, ready to leave. And once again I keep finding stop signs on the roads, saying, "Where do you think you're going. You're not finished, kid." Telling me to stay and stop and go, all at once.

I am torn between the will to be seen and the will to stay hidden, but there is something in the way he, or this, or that, makes me feel okay. A bit better every day.

As long as I keep doing my part, which is simply to keep doing—breathing, inhale, exhale—I know that my heart will do its part, and I will go on well.

I believe in the constant flow of life.
The way it always pulls me back.

Nature

Don't forget that the land is always out there, making its way, doing everything it can so you can breathe fresh air; so you can eat fresh food; so you can move and see and feel and think, and it's on your side. The world is out there doing what it's been doing way before you came here. It's firm and strong and it takes a lot to bring it down.

So from time to time, just go outside and look at this spectacle. This pure painting right in front of your eyes. No one created it. No one owns it. It doesn't want anything. It doesn't need to prove anything to anyone. It simply is.

So maybe, try a little tenderness. Just give it a chance to do what it can do. Just let it help you

breathe

and eat

and move

and see,

and maybe try to live your life in a way that doesn't kill this force of nature that is just trying to give you a world worth living in. A clean world. A fresh world.

Paths, forests, oceans, animals, oxygen, water. That's all it takes.

Just try a little tenderness towards this world we've been lucky enough to build our homes in.

If you take care of it, it will take care of you.

My Mind it Travels

There is something that happens when you land in a new place, walking new streets, seeing new faces. It's something in the way you view the ordinary. The ordinary becomes interesting and strange and magnificent. The small daily tasks or habits are noticed, and ordinary smells, sights and tastes become wonderfully alive. You realise how you've built patterns all around yourself, closing you in, and you haven't even noticed. From the first thing you do when you wake up, to when you think you need to eat, and how you choose to spend your day. The simple way of putting one foot in front of the other changes and you walk in a different way, as if every step is the start of something new and incredible, because it in fact is, or could be, and it's all about how you choose to view it.

I close in on myself and my mind, shut people out and distract myself with this body of work I'm trying to build. A way of choosing to ignore the real world in order to be in my own, because the real one seems too harsh and I never found a way to simply fit.

But then you move, or leave, or simply flee, and the moment of waking up isn't a struggle anymore. You don't let the alarm clock ring for fifteen minutes before you drag yourself to do your daily tasks with no heart. Suddenly, you open your eyes before the world is awake and your heart is already excited and beating faster than ever before and you just smile because, what is there not to smile about? You make your way through new streets, taking buses with destinations you don't know the names of because there is no destination, it's all about the next step and where it can lead. The way your feet don't drag anymore, as if the concrete in this place makes it easier to just make your way through the day and you don't even notice how tired your legs are after walking for twelve hours, before you finally rest your head with a smile on your face and a thousand new pictures, smells and sounds spinning around, and you can't wait to wake up in a few hours and get to do it all over again. The same small familiar things, but in different ways, every second, because the familiar becomes unfamiliar in the mind of a traveller. And it's not about the big journey around the world, but about small changes in patterns. The letting go of habits, routines and how things are supposed to be, because there's no such thing. No such thing as how you or your surroundings or daily life are supposed to be. Sometimes you just need to trust the process. It's on your side and always has been. You've just been too busy to notice, to feel and jump straight in, but it's your time now. Your time.

I spend mornings writing to the smell of coffee from a small local coffee shop, and it's how the barista wish you good morning in a language you don't understand, so you smile and that's enough because humans are humans and we're all the same, making our own ways, (we're all on our way).
You have nothing to fear. No one is more in the right place than you are.
Now go.

Go. Go. Go.

Hometown Blues

It's summer and we're driving in your father's car with the windows down. My hand stretched out, forming waves with the speed. It's July and the roads are cracked.

We were collections of characters, divided into groups of "hipsters", "artsy", "academics" and "athletes". But I couldn't care less. I belonged to no group and no person, and I was not interested in fitting in or out. I just wanted to sit on my mountain a little bit away, observing it all, laughing a bit, wishing I was involved, sometimes.

The times have changed but they are still the same, and we're driving the same road with the same music, laughing at the same jokes. You go your rounds and crack some hearts, and by the end of every circle we're back where we started. Different, yes, but all the same.

This hometown blues is a summer day and the roads are cracked and dry.

London

London is loud. London is greedy. It's busy and fast and I find myself following the crowd with hectic steps, hurrying to no-one-knows-where and people never look where they're going. Their feet touch the ground but they don't feel it, just keep running, and the people on the tube turn into empty bodies, looking straight ahead or angrily at the person who stole the last seat.

But London is also alive. Never lonely. Never still. Never bored. I find myself wanting to wake up before the sunrise to not miss the first hours of the day because the day starts early here. And I find myself walking the streets long into midnight, because the day never ends here and people are going somewhere. I'm not sure where, but at least they're going and that's the only point sometimes, and I find myself wanting to go somewhere here, too. Somehow it doesn't really matter in which direction or for how long because you always end up somewhere and there is always somewhere to go.

Musicians and writers with large dreams come here to fulfil them. They hustle their way through hours of tubes and streets with heavy equipment just to play for three people and a sound guy with no compensation. Maybe one of those three people will be someone of importance, who can make a difference. Musicians and writers with large dreams do this year after year and maybe one or two of them eventually happen to be in the right place at the right time and someone gives them a hand or two, but most of us simply move on.

You don't leave London behind, you don't forget about it. You carry it with you wherever you go and it will teach you for the rest of your life. On nights when you can't sleep, many years from now, you will recall the conversation with the bartender somewhere in Camden, where you played a few songs, because people always play a few songs somewhere in Camden. And you will remember the kind bus driver who let you go on the last night bus even though your oyster card was empty, and you will remember the noisy streets at 3 a.m., walking home with someone who's as lonely and lost as you are, because everyone is here. You will think about the people you met and left and never saw again, and you will wonder how they are. What they're doing now. Are they still in the city? Still hustling with heavy equipment on tubes, unable to pay their rent?

You don't leave London behind, you simply carry it with you and move on. And when you come back to walk these streets in years to come, you will walk them in wonder, thinking, *did I really live here? or did I simply exist?* The answer is: I still don't know but I'm glad I did, whatever it was I did, because I carry it with me and it's still teaching me. About discipline. About the eagerness to survive. About hard work and never asking for more, just trying to put in one good day after another, one good gig or song, practice or session after the other, and maybe one day it will lead somewhere. I think it did lead me somewhere and I think you don't notice that until you're back walking the circle. You need to break it, but it's a nice circle.

I think it did lead me somewhere, and God, am I thankful to have made it here, wherever that is.

The start of everything

I don't know,
it might just be the summer deceiving my senses, or all these new books I read, or all these new words I learn, but I'm becoming someone I'm not yet familiar with
and it keeps my eyes open wide.
It might just be June and simple mornings
or the way he says my name
or the way I stay up late
waiting for a word or two, as a small reminder of being known,
but I am becoming someone I'm not yet familiar with, and it's quite a wonderful feeling. It's like the first day in a new city and every road is a new adventure, leading to something new. I catch myself in the mirror, making movements and thinking thoughts I never once did, and it's quite a different thing, the discovery of myself, from a different side of the sea. A different side of me,
for I've been lonely and angry, at myself and everyone else
but there was this day, this spring, when all fell into place and I took a breath and let things go.
I took a breath and let it go
and suddenly the air was crisper
and my lungs lighter
and suddenly
there was him
saying my name
in different ways
and I catch myself throwing glances in the mirror,
seeing someone I don't know quite yet
but I can't wait to,
and that's the start of everything.

Journal VIIII

March 2018

Home at last

Growing up is a wonderful thing to do. Tracing the years back, looking at myself like someone else, someone different. I was angry and anxious, wanting to prove the whole world wrong, prove myself wrong, prove that I could be anything I wanted to be and I was gonna show them all.

I was driven by external forces, wanting everyone to see me like this and think of me like that. I planned my words carefully, my clothes, my songs so that the world would see me from the right angle.

It's different now. I'm different now. I don't spin the chair anymore. I rest peacefully with both eyes steady, listening and caring. I don't rush through the rain with a rucksack, but instead say, "Let's have another coffee, tell me one more story," and I wait out the rain.

I'm no longer driven by external forces, but internal ones. I no longer care what the world sees me as. Instead I care about what I think of myself. How I feel, here, now, hands on my heart. Am I peaceful? Am I calm? Am I content? Lonely? Wise? Do I sit steady, do I listen, do I care?

I want to care. I want to be someone who cares genuinely about people and places, the climate and health. I want to care about my pace and my body, my days and my work. My work … the only thing I've ever had. My books and my songs, my journey on this endless road and I love it still, the constant tugging, wanting to reach a little deeper, create a little better. Lovelier, with grace.

I want to be a woman of integrity, walking strong and sure no matter where and I want to talk in a way that draws people in. I want to lower my voice, look people straight in the eyes and talk to their heart, like they're the only ones that matter for me in this very second because I want to be someone who sees people. Who cares. Who helps. Who can reach out a hand and say, "You're not alone." I want to leave everyone I meet feeling a little better about themselves and I want to make people excited about their own lives and journeys. I want to make people feel special, like they matter, like they always do. Everyone has a story to tell and I want to hear them —I want to hear it all.

I want to be a woman who paved her own path and who knows failure and heartache but who kept going anyway because it made her wiser. It made her smarter and stronger, but also softer and kinder. I want to be the one you turn to for guidance and comfort. I want to create things that become a source of stability for people, some sort of home. Write books that you read until the edges are torn and songs that you listen to in your headphones on a lonely night bus, taking you somewhere far, far away.

I want to be so sure of my own place in the universe that no one could ever doubt me. What I'm about or what I'm here to do. I want to be a safe aura in a sea of worries and uncertainty. I want to stand for clarity where only chaos seems to grow.

Growing up is a wonderful thing. I can feel myself expanding quietly.

A STILLNESS IN MY TROUBLED MIND

I found a stillness in my troubled mind.
The steady rhythm of my heart, my chest, the seasons of everything,
and I'm learning to acknowledge the cycles of the moon. Where I am towards it all,
my position in between the earth and the sky, the gods and the rest.
Only I can take that place.
I made a peaceful ceremony of watching the full moon at midnight,
putting my right hand over my chest, saying,
"I will trust you to carry me, if you trust me to carry you."

I found a stillness in my troubled mind.

Evening prayer

I pray not for much, but for things with great weight.
I pray for strength to get up, tomorrow and the day after the next day.
I pray for clarity in thought, to know where to put that strength, these gifts, second by second.
I pray for something to move me, a thought or a dream, a poem even. Something to grab me at heart, make that clock in my chest beat louder,
make me put those shoes on and go after it.

I rest peacefully in my uneasiness, devour the sweet memories or longings. A sadness
for something that hasn't happened yet
but I know it might, soon, one day,
and it's a heavy feeling, yes it is. Like a black stone in your chest, sinking deeper and heavier the lonelier you are, the quieter it gets.
But then the softness that surrounds you when you think *you can sleep now. close your eyes. you've done enough for today. you did just fine.*

I rest peacefully in my uneasiness.

I whisper a quiet prayer to the loving voice within me, to show up a little more often. To please come tomorrow again, please be here...? I whisper a quiet goodnight to friends long lost, but who I still think of as friends, if I would see them on the street tomorrow. For I don't have a lot left, so the things I do have I value more.
I sing a hymn for the lands out there that I will one day wander. The many seas I am yet to sail. I sing myself to sleep, like so many others, and I pray that one day I will meet them. Those who made me pull

through nights like these, again and again, knowing there are others out there, like me.

I rest in ease, knowing there are others out there, whispering themselves to sleep, just like me.

Journal X

April 2018

by the ocean….

I outgrew my story. I've outgrown my songs and books and path and dream.
You outgrow bands and loves, people and cities, and that's okay. I'm learning that part of growing up is learning how to leave things behind that no longer belong to you. Behaviours and values, but also interests and passions. You might find yourself in an in-between phase, where you're outgrowing your path but still don't know where to enter your new one. Or you might find yourself having outgrown your passion, without having found a new one. Your dream does not belong to you anymore. The butterflies are gone and the glory of the finish-line seems more like a grey cloud, something you no longer aspire to reach. This is okay.

The most impactful moments of my life have been the clean ones. The clean streets in the early a.m. hours—the town is mine to own. The blank pages—no story yet written. The new friendship, the new name, the new pair of eyes staring into mine and I can be whoever I want from now on.

Growing up takes time and effort, lessons and heartache, and I am proud to have been documenting my questions and attempted answers since my teenage years. I created something. A character of sorts, but she seemed as real as me and maybe I tried to become like her. Maybe I wanted to be like her. Maybe I tried to live up to the image I drew, the pure unworldly consciousness of "The Glass Child". Maybe it was a dream. Someone I aspired to be seen as.

Someone I turned to for guidance. "What would The Glass Child do?" Maybe it was a cape. A costume of magical colors I could hide my shattered identity under, so as not to feel so detached. To not have to explain myself. Who's Charlotte? Who cares, this is The Glass Child! I felt no responsibility because The Glass Child didn't have to answer. She just did. Half alive. Half person, half fiction. She thought and felt and wrote and sang but did not live.
Maybe it was everything I could never be. Maybe it was everything I ever could be.

But I am a few miles more travelled. I am a few years wiser. My heart has been running and beating, stopping and fighting and now I find it calm. Beating like a steady clock on the wall, tick/tock, knowing its stubborn ways because I tried to fight it for so many years but it kept on beating and now I respect it. I thank it.

I respect my people, because I never took care of them. I never kept in touch, only left and took for granted and I've been selfish and angry at everyone and everything because I've felt useless and hopeless and I wanted someone's attention, someone to tell me, "YOU DID IT! I SEE YOU! I ACKNOWLEDGE YOUR STRUGGLE AND PRAISE YOUR ACHIEVEMENTS AND I NO LONGER LOOK DOWN ON YOU!"
But people have their own stories and no one cares as much as you do. People get bored. I get bored too, of myself and my name. The Glass Child became like the costume I had to wear because I created it and I wore it with pride some days, with embarrassment on others.

I had to fall into detours. A few rounds back and forth, trying this and failing that. Maybe I could be this and maybe I could do that. I tried many jobs, many careers, many people. Left many interests but

explored many too. And all this, all the missteps and years of feeling failed and under-accomplished, I can see now coming through in my music.
My voice has changed. The melodies it creates. The chords that intrigue me. And for the very first time in many, many years I write songs that make me feel proud. For simply creating them. I sit back and feel *this is it. That's it. This thing. It's IT.*
Maybe I only felt it once before. The very first times I wrote songs, back then, over ten years ago. I felt that. I created my songs from pure innocence and it made me feel real. Then it went missing but I kept on going and now I feel faceless with no expectations because I'm nobody and have no name to live up to and I write songs with eyes closed and I sit back and feel this is it. What's my name? Band name? Brand name? Website?
Who cares, this is my song. This is how I sound and this is how I look. I can sing it to you, here and now, and I won't need any effects or a band because this is it and I have a voice. Yes? No? I'll sing anyway. You can leave if you want to, I'll be here singing because that's what I do. Now. After all these years. Turn the mic off, I'll sing anyway.

Growing up takes time and effort, but it's a wonderful journey and I'm proud to have taken on the challenge. I'm embarrassed for things I've said. I'm sorry for people I've left. But I'm determined to be better. To turn myself into someone good. A woman of integrity. I no longer want to act out of naiveté or anger, I want to live up to this "The Glass Child" I could never be, but from a new light. A less fictionalised one. A real one.

This is me, in every way I can ever be. The Glass Child is in me, I think. She came from me. But there is also a little more here now. Not so empty. A little more … real.

I still have hope in who I am becoming.

The Gift of Now

May I propose to you, a new way of thinking?
May I offer an alternate way of speed?

I'd say:
Where do you stand right now? Stop for a second. Look around. Are you inside, four walls, a door, a window? Or maybe outside? Sky, fresh air, white noise?
Maybe the ground is even, smooth. Or is it filled with cracks and bolts, making your feet form in a wonderfully human way,
and what can you hear? Close your eyes. Find yourself in the middle of nature's orchestra. A bird high up in the sky. A car somewhere far away. A child; a mother; someone making coffee on the other side of the wall.
Now notice the light. Is it bright, dark, grey? A natural sunlight, reflecting in the bakery window. Or is it mellow, compressed and comfortable?

I'd say: during these last three minutes that you stood there, simply being, simply noticing—did you once think about the worry that was nagging in your chest this morning? Did you once think about the laundry, the post, the bills to pay in four months?
It is said that there are only two possible things in this entire universe that can actually cause you trouble; only two possible reasons for all your worries and sorrow.
The first one is regrets about the past, and the second is worries about the future. Two factors which are completely out of your control.

Let me repeat:
The only two possible factors that can cause you troubles and worries, in this entire universe, are two factors that in this moment are completely out of your control.

xx x xxx

May I propose to you a new way of thinking:
Maybe, if we can learn to be a little bit more here, now, where we stand at this very moment—leave the past behind and take the future with ease when it shows up—we'd have a little bit more peace and quiet to find space to smile; to understand and experience every second of the day.
We miss so much by the haze of being somewhere else, in our heads.

Make a little more space to take in what you already have.
Today is a wonderful day to be alive.

Natural spectacle

… And isn't the world a treasure in itself? A spectacle glittering every single day, without concern if anyone's watching or not. It simply goes on, elegantly, letting nature have its way.

We only need to open our eyes to witness the biggest masterpiece ever created.
The ticket is already in your hand.

This is what it's about:

It's about waking up by yourself, no alarms or electrical sounds, on a Sunday morning to a clear blue sky. It's about being too tired to go to your friend's birthday party, wishing you could just stay home, safe inside. But it's about showing up anyway, knowing that it means something for someone and it's about knowing that you mean something to someone. It's about the white flakes of snow an early morning in December. How you can breathe it in and let it go. How New Year's Eve is always a letdown unless you take it as it comes and realise that if you are happy where you are, with people you love, nothing more is needed. It's about the fight with your parents, how they'll never understand, but how you love them anyway, despite it all. It's about knowing that there are millions of unexplored interests, hobbies and new passions out there for you to discover and devour. It's about the startups that fail and fold and the starting again, the people who leave and hearts that break but also how we can learn to love again. And it's about the radio hosts who say good morning in the same tone every day for ten years and how you will miss them when they're exchanged with someone new, someone younger, saying good morning in a foreign way. It's about the libraries. Big open houses full of hundreds of books by the greatest people and thinkers this world has ever seen, free for you to read and learn from and take in and consume. How magical! It's about the 3 a.m. call from the hospital, telling you they got there too late. How you stare into the abyss and can't see how you will be able to exist in this place, this planet, without her. It's about putting one foot in front of the other and simply going on, anyway, and it's about waking up a year from now and realising that you actually did go on, despite it all.

It's about catching glimpses in the mirror on days you feel beautiful, just as you are, and it's about the days you want to hide beneath ten layers of clothing and not meet anyone or anything, and it's about being okay with both.

It's about the switch in perspective, shifting the "oh" to "ah" and seeing uncertainty as exciting. The not knowing what will happen as curiosity, for everything is in fact interesting if you are interested enough and I know for sure that life is not always oceans and blue skies, but I also know for sure that at any given moment there are a thousand beautiful things to find comfort in. I know for sure that when you strip it down, undress life to its very core, it's the small unchanged things that will stand certain like a rock in the sea, and you shall find your way back there whenever the weather gets rough.

It's about the undesigned things, raw and real. Natural and pure. The feeling of crisp air on your skin. The way no matter how many times your heart breaks or dreams fail, the sea will stand sure and pure and you will find your way back there.

You will find strength in the certainty of the sea.

A HOME ON THE ROAD

I'll never tire of singing. To get to sit in front of alert eyes and do the only thing I'll never doubt. Play with the syllables, rhythms, and stories. I get to reshape and recreate new meanings to the same words. See how they're dragged in, slowly, all quiet now: I've got them by the heartstrings, I can do anything I please.
To know that they are listening, to me, right now. So don't worry. Just close your eyes, do your thing. You made it here. You're here!
I'll never tire of the moment during a concert when the audience switch from being a little uncomfortable because it's too intimate, too intense, never been here before—to embracing it. Embracing everything about my songs, my story, this evening and each other. By the end of each night, we're all talking freely and enthusiastically about life and journeys, sharing dreams and growing up. It's something about the intimacy that makes people open up. Here is my story, my journey, my very bare heart.
Now show me yours.

I have an urge to strip my life down to the bare bones to get to the core of it. I get tense and angry, accumulating layers around my essential needs, covering up my passions. These layers cover up my marks and scars, bones and weary heart and I want it to show because sometimes I feel my only purpose here is to say *pretty little girl, keep going, you're doing just fine.* And I'd like to be an example of no matter how dark and thick and hopeless it feels, for years maybe, things can and will change. If you want them to. If you're determined to make them do so. Because I'm in my twenties and I laugh and sing and spend my days doing things that matter so much to me that I'm giving up comfort and pay-checks, but I'd like everyone to know that it wasn't always like this. I wasn't always like

this.
I was the girl in a grey hoodie slamming the door at midnight because I'd had enough. I was the girl not knowing how to speak or walk or pave my way through schools and family dilemmas, and I never had friends because how can you when you're not a friend to yourself and I just needed salvation. So I smoked and drank and starved and ran, escaped in any way I could, just wanting to find a way.

I'm not sure that I found a way, exactly, but I saw a sign like a light in the sky and I followed it religiously. I followed the small, broken signals telling me that "this is what you're good at and this is what makes you smile" and I went after it. Determined to create a life for myself that made me excited to wake up.

I didn't necessarily find a way, but I created one. And I'd like to be an example for how you can, too. To show, with my actions, that systems and norms of how to build careers and a living are just made up by lazy people who never cared enough to question it or spend much time creating their own map. Don't follow this passive system. Don't buy the rule book of how to be a singer, a photographer, an actor, a business owner. Observe. Read. Be smart. Practice. Learn the skills and principles, your industry and how people before you made it, and then create your own unique world made up of all things that intrigue you. Not only will you find yourself with a life created only for you, you will also find that you never have to feel competition with friends or people around you, because you're doing something different. You're doing your own thing. You're unique. One of a kind. And so, people will cheer you on, saying "How cool is that!" and you will admire and respect the people next to you but still stand tall on your path because

it
was
made
for
you.

So I guess I'm not done yet, like I've thought so many times. I still have things to tell and teach and learn and preach and I never want to act pretentious, like I have it all figured out (because I don't). I would simply like to experiment with this thing called "life". How you can live it, how you can build it, how you can make a complete U-turn and still be fine. And maybe by doing so in my own way and at my own pace, someone out there, maybe you, can find a tiny spark of hope to find your own unique path because sometimes, I'm thinking that what I'm missing in this world is people who speak with fire and excitement, about things they believe in and fight for. I want people with life in their eyes. Untired heroes, eager to live.

So find your own combination of things to learn and see and be passionate about. Learn from everyone but be your own guidance, and you will find a red-hot feeling in your chest each night, eager for the possibilities of a new day. No one knows your heart as well as you do.

I still have a lot to do. I still have a lot to say.
I'm still on my way.

Reintroduce Yourself

Let's reintroduce ourselves.

Pretend you're not here anymore, but there, where your mind sometimes wanders, wherever that may be. Maybe a different continent, a different town, another place.
Or exactly where you are but living with a different name, a different job, a different boyfriend, girlfriend, wife.
Or maybe everything is exactly the way you want it to be
but still,
let us reintroduce ourselves.

Let me explain:
The world moves fast and we make our ways every day on our own even though we live with others and tell them things. We all see the world through our own eyes
and hear things, feel things, think things
and my day moves slowly when yours is fast
and we have little time for reflection.
But the hand he shook a year ago does not belong to me anymore,
and the way you said your name that day is not how you say it now.
We change and grow up but people around take us for granted. They think they know all there is to know, forgetting that you are a universe, expanding every single day
and sometimes it surfaces
and he says,
"You're different. You're changed."
As if it's a bad thing, something to be avoided.
But I am here to tell you it's not.

I woke up this morning, early like I always do, alone on a small island, where I went to to rearrange and start anew. It's summer so the sun is up before me and it's quite magical. I've made it a holy ritual, sitting cross-legged on the floor, listening to the stillness from living a bit outside. I hear the boats from the port, just close enough,
and there's a cat looking for food outside my door
and sometimes I fall asleep with the window wide open,
wishing to wake up with the pace of nature
and it's all just simple and easy and so right.

I've made it a holy ritual to sit there,
with the simplicity of not a lot and it's more than enough.
No plans or thoughts or needs,
and you might think it's unproductive, lazy or boring,
but see, I used to hurry and run and breathe without filling my lungs
and my head was spinning and I had to lie down several times a day
and people used to tell me "That is not normal"
but I kept on running
with nowhere to run
and it was exhausting.

Anyway, I've done this every morning since I came here, a quiet part of the Greek island Paros, but this morning something happened.
I was sitting in my usual way when I suddenly twisted my head and caught a reflection of a girl in the window and I made a sudden move because I thought I was alone but there she was and I was caught by surprise. I just sat there, staring at the reflection of that girl, and I tried to recognise the lines in her face and her eyes and her ways, and it felt strange and unfamiliar but still familiar, and these things used to scare me. They used to make me run the other way

and turn the volume up and scream my name louder everywhere so no one could misunderstand or mistake me. My ways and my self
but I am older now.
And wiser, maybe, so I took a deep breath and tried to understand her. I looked at her, and she looked at me. Her eyes were kind but shy and her smile was too, but at least she did smile. She looked curious and excited, for what I don't know, but there she was and it felt strange but real. Real, like something you find under layers of peel and protection, under make-up or editing.

I sat there for some time, waiting for something to happen, but I'm learning that other people rarely make a move and things are up to you if you want them to happen. So, I discussed, loud but mature, told myself that I can just ignore her. Act foreign and keep her hidden from everyone else. Hide her smile and firm mind for she felt unfamiliar and new
but something told me that she was not meant to stay hidden,
stored away like a shadow,
for she looked real
and real things are rare
and hard to find
and when you do you should shelter them.
Treat them like treasures
and the *me* in my head suddenly felt old and out of date.
So I stood up, spoke out loud though just to myself and said,
"I'd like to reintroduce myself". That was that and so I did.

And now here I am, writing to you to let me reintroduce myself. To my town, to my mom, to my friends, to the moon. To my past and my faults, my strengths and my baggage. To my old neighbour I still

write to and the teachers I sometimes pass, to you and them and all the rest, but most importantly, to myself.
To my mind and my thoughts and the mirror on the wall,
because sometimes I see myself and think "That's not me" or "Where have I gone?" when I have simply evolved
and moved on, grown up and above.

So I dare you to reintroduce yourself.
To your brother, to your mom, to your husband, to yourself or to me. What I want to know is,
who are you now? After all those years?

Who are you
really
now?

How do you look? Really? Without knowing your style from the past.
How do you live? Really? Without knowing where you grew up.
What do you love? Now? Without knowing what you might have loved, once.

How do you walk? Talk? Dress?
I don't care about the program you chose to study
or the books you used to read
or the boy you used to love
a year ago, a month ago — tell me what these things turned you into
and what they still teach you now?

Or maybe more importantly, if we were to meet in a month, in a year or two years,
who would you like to introduce yourself as?

Who would you like to be?
How would you like me to know you?

How do you look?
A new haircut,
a smaller apartment
in the middle of New York?
With big windows from floor to ceiling
or a little red house
out in the countryside?
With a front porch, where you drink freshly brewed coffee to the sound of stillness every morning,
and you could have a garden
where only flowers grow with no thorns,
and you can watch them bloom
a little more every day
just like you do.

Bloom
a little more
every day.
Just like you do.

So let's reintroduce ourselves.
To the world.
To ourselves.
To each other.
There are a thousand different worlds to live in during one lifetime
and why settle for one world
when there are so many wonderful ones.

My personality should not be taken for granted and I wish people asked my name and what I do and why I do it
every time they meet me,
because what I told you yesterday
is not, and should not, be the same today
and that is called growing.
So let us grow.
With each and with every breath,
and let us do it wildly
and shamelessly
like the flowers bloom in April,
and let us reintroduce ourselves to the world
and let the world reintroduce itself to us
every day as the sun goes up,
for we should never take it for granted
or think that we know it
or think it knows us.
Maybe it's not as sad
or dark
or heartbroken
as it was last spring,
and maybe if you looked with new eyes each morning, as you opened the window, as if the world was a stranger you're yet to get to know, you would discover that the hatred, or sadness, or resistance it once gave you was another world, and this is a new one. A wiser one. A brighter one.
Maybe we're all learning and growing and changing,
and maybe this could be just another new beginning,
leading somewhere magnificent.

So I dare you to reintroduce yourself. Write me a letter. Long or short, happy or sad, whatever you like, but don't tell me where you've been. Tell me where you are or where you want to be a year from now, for that is all that matters. That is all I care about.

Write your reintroduction to theglasschildmusic@gmail.com with the subject line "Reintroduction – Your Name (or desired name)", and we'll create a big beautiful collection of reintroductions. As a group, a tribe, a family, where we all can be exactly who we are or would like to be now, this very second.
I'm waiting for you.

My name is Charlotte

I write stories, create worlds and dress my days in pretty melodies. Sometimes I turn them into books. Sometimes I turn them into songs. I produce records, publish books, and try to make it matter to someone while doing it. My belief is that you can become exactly who you want to become, and do exactly whatever you want to do, if you just want it bad enough. I believe in creating your own life. Sculpt it like a masterpiece. Write it like a poem.

I believe in happiness.

I am a teacher and I am a student. I read more than I speak and I speak less then I think. I don't want to be a writer or a songwriter for the sake of being called so—I want to live my life to the magnificent limit, and then capture and tell about it.

I've had some successes, I've had a lot of failures, and I am still learning. I've been completely broke. Woken up with no idea how to afford food for the day, and I also know comfortable living with more than enough. Happiness, motivation and excitement have nothing to do with how much I own.

I am a minimalist to the core. I feel best when I know I can fit everything I own in one rucksack and a guitar case. Simplicity and discipline are my saviours. I don't wish to be a part of materialism and consumerism and I don't believe in holidays. If you need to take a holiday from your own life, I don't think you're spending your days doing what you love. A lot of people don't agree with me, and if you're one of them, I still respect you. I will try to understand you, if you try to understand me.

I'm a daughter and I'm a sister. I'm no one's best friend and no one is my best friend. I call strangers family because if you can give me one moment of precious memory, I love you.

I've practiced meditation for five years, and I am slowly healing my worried mind. I consider old philosophers like Marcus Aurelius and Joseph Campbell my mentors and they're teaching me what it means to live.

Some of my favorite writers are Jack Gilbert, Fernando Pessoa and Anton Chekhov. Sometimes I read something, or hear something, and my whole stomach turns inside out because poetry and art have an impact on me. It hurts that I cannot write like that myself and I'm never as alive as when I write something that just fits inside this empty space in my chest.

I'm a runner and I've been running for as long as I can remember. At least 45 km every week, all year long. That gives me a lot of time to think about stuff. I like the way there's nothing but my mind, my thoughts, the music in my ears and the next step. The world is closed off and my only mission for the next hour or two is to simply take another step with another breath. I think running is a metaphor for a lot of things, and I think it's teaching me a lot. Like how to beat that voice in your head, telling you that you're tired, that you can't go on, that you want to stop. How to beat it and learn how to go on anyway, and realise that your body is capable of so much more than you ever thought. How to push yourself to do things you never thought you could, and how to always be improving—always be pushing yourself. I know it's just running but it's also not just running because it's about how I'd like to live my life. To never give up simply because my head tells me to.

I practice yoga and I do it without wanting to achieve anything, which is the goal with yoga, and that's why it's been hard. I have a hard time doing things if it won't lead anywhere, if it won't teach me something or develop into something or give me an outcome. But yoga and meditation are just what they are. That's why it's teaching me to simply be. me. here. now. and be okay with that.

I value my friends like my family, mostly because I have a hard time finding friends who stay. Or maybe I'm the one who never stays. Either way, I value the people around me and I'm still trying to learn how to be a good person, a good friend, because I'm mostly not. I'm mostly selfish. But I have hope in myself.

I've been many "me's", and I'm still trying to figure things out. But I think I'm learning that the whole "figuring it out" is the thing, it's life, and nothing to be rushed. I aim to be a lifelong student and a lifelong learner.

I want to write music that makes your heart turn inside out. I want to shelter and build up storms. I want to be found on a stage somewhere far away, with my guitar and my voice, and I want someone who doesn't know me to find me on that stage that night when he or she needs it the most. I want to make someone's world disappear for a minute or two because I simply sang with my heart on my sleeve, and I want to be known for my art. Known for my words, my stories and my visions.
I want to write poetry and prose, essays and novels. I want to publish books that travel the world and end up on a worn-out bookshelf somewhere I've never been, and I wish to be named in the same sentences as the writers and artists I consider myself raised and influenced by.

I am easily bored, but I am also easily contented by small means. Like a few close friends, a bottle of wine and a conversation about something that matters. Or a walk in a foreign city by myself, taking in new sounds and views. Kicking leaves off the ground with a slow acoustic song in my headphones, or waking up to a new day with a clear dream in mind, to go after and fulfil.

I have a lot left to do and see and learn and feel, and I am trying to be fully aware as I do it. I am learning as I go along, and I guess that you are too, and I want to experience this path together with you. Because we can all use a hand to hold, some days, some nights. We're all in this together.

Love always,
Charlotte

INDEX

ABOUT THE AUTHOR

Charlotte Eriksson is a songwriter and author from Sweden, currently living somewhere in Europe, wherever the music plays at the moment. She left everything she had and knew as a teenager, and moved to England to create a life for herself that made her excited to wake up in the morning. Since then she has started her own artist collective *Broken Glass Records*, written four books (*Empty Roads & Broken Bottles; in search for The Great Perhaps, Another Vagabond Lost To Love, You're Doing Just Fine,* and *Everything changed when I forgave myself*), and released 7 EPs and 3 LPs under the artist name The Glass Child. Her writings have been published on sites like Thought Catalog, Bella Grace Magazine and Rebelle Society.

AUTHOR NOTE

As a small independent author, I write books for the pure fulfilment of connecting with souls out there, who might be like me. Who might recognise themselves in my story. The thought that my words might mean something to someone out there is what keeps me going during my dark days.

If you have found any joy or comfort in my words, please don't be shy … Say hi to me online, send me a picture of you and this book, tag me on instagram, or tell me about a memory you'll never forget.

If you want to help me tell the world about my books and story, it would mean the whole universe if you wanted to write a few nice words about this book as a review on Amazon & Goodreads. Tell all your friends and family about it. Share your favorite quote from the book on instagram, tumblr, twitter … Tag me so I can find you! But most of all, go out and take your place in the world, for only you can fill it. Together we can make the world a better place.

Thank you for being you.

I have three other books called:
You're Doing Just Fine
Another Vagabond Lost To Love
and
Empty Roads & Broken Bottles; in search for The Great Perhaps
You can read all about them on my website
www.CharlotteEriksson.com
There you will also find excerpts, quotes and some pictures from the books.

www.Twitter.com/justaglasschild
www.Instagram.com/justaglasschild
www.facebook.com/TheGlassChild
www.TheGlassChild.tumblr.com
www.Youtube.com/aglasschild
theglasschildmusic@gmail.com

You can get signed copies of all my books, signed CDs, merch and other creations in my online store: www.TheGlassChild.bigcartel.com

If you want to support me to keep creating music and write books, I'd like to invite you to join me on Patreon: www.Patreon.com/TheGlassChild

Love always,
Charlotte

This book is possible thanks to ...

This book exists and is possible thanks to my supporters, funders and ambassadors who make up my publishing house, management, record label and support family on Patreon:

Ralph Walther
Li Hoon Kong
Casey Mitchell
John Deal
Samson Wu
Alex Currie
Donatus Bonke
Mark Chandler
Andy W Marsden
Jens Hohmuth
Stuart Kewish
Jean-Paul
Danielle Lejeune
Justin Warren
Julie Patterson
Vinny Sheridan
Maxime Dehuit
Christer Isaksson
Mario Rauchfuß
Glenn Sargent
Squirrel
Joe Booth
Douglas LaFreniere
Alain Kohli
Steve Collins
Ryan O'Gorman
Hanna Olofsson
Brian Patterson
Brian Bolvin
Calisa Lesser
Andy Rodriguez
Paul Moosmann
Schylar Raye
Garrison Pledger
Robert Webber
Amanda Hurley
Peter Mitchell
Peyton E Smith
Natacha Dauphin
Scott Sandler
John Hartil
Katarina Waters
Andreas Laemmermann
Jim Boere
Daniela Șerban
Angie Cormier
Kristin Sapelak
John Malone
Emil Josefsson
Paul Mathews
Samuel Lillywhite
John Aylott
Nicola Tirrell
Dan Balkwill
Randy L Dienes
Claire LaVelle
Steve Zwolinski
Ian Hall
Joshua Koppinger
Alain Delanay
Rachel Mattick
Carman Zygadlo
Nadezhda Narina
Nikola Pejchinoski
Wolfgang Uka
Mark Cousens
Ian Robinson
Jacques Szluha
Kevin Kirk
Stephen Westberg
Ruben P. H.
Irenio Canales
Chantel Brown
Chrissy Akers
Kathrin Yuki
Craig Black
Craig Sinclair
Cooper George
Peter Karlsson
Alex Hjelmaas
David West
Joao Duarte
Julia Marie Aguilar
Michele Jade
Doğukan Şahin
Ruby June Corah
Larry Kamp
Kaz Lewinski
Matt Canton
Christina Korosec
Димитър Черкезов
Sophie Grainger
Bridget Robertson
Sharon Strunk
Cosmin
Casandra Wagner
Emmeline

Special thanks to my Executive Producers:

Ralph Walther & Stuart Kewish

Printed in Poland
by Amazon Fulfillment
Poland Sp. z o.o., Wrocław

51451919R00078